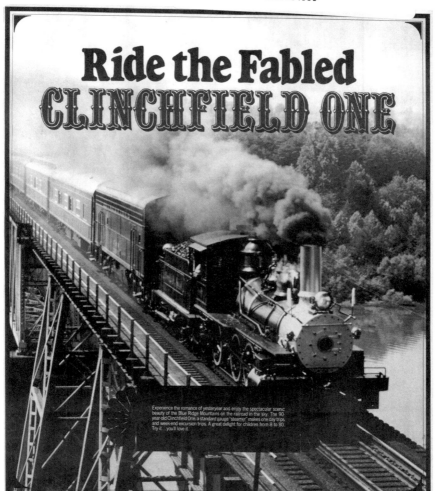

In 1972, this promotional poster was printed to celebrate "the railroad in the sky." Ticket sales were booming and getting national publicity. T.D. Moore's dream was moving full steam ahead. *Image courtesy of Mike Tilley.*

To: Stuart Watson
Enjoy the book!

THE
CLINCHFIELD
~ No. 1 ~

Tennessee's
LEGENDARY
STEAM ENGINE

MARK A. STEVENS & A.J. "ALF" PEOPLES

Charleston ╟ London
THE
History
PRESS

Published by The History Press
Charleston, SC 29403
www.historypress.net

First published 2014

Manufactured in the United States

ISBN 978.1.62619.596.7
Library of Congress CIP data applied for.

From Mark: To the people in my life who always believe in me: my wife and No. 1 best friend, Amy; my parents, Amos and Peggy Stevens; and my brother, Bryan. And to my very good dog, Rue, who kept me company during long days of writing and research.

From Alf: To my daughter, Sarah, and her husband, Justin; my grandson, Jackson, and my granddaughter on the way, Avery Elizabeth; my sister Carolyn and her husband, Phil; and my sister Lana and her husband, Harvey, all of whom took care of me and everything I needed so I could work on this book.

CONTENTS

ACKNOWLEDGEMENTS

Special thanks to Thelma Conrad, executive director of the Cass County, Indiana Historical Society; David Crockett of Rocky Mount, North Carolina; David and Charlotte DeVault of Kingsport, Tennessee; Micah Epps and Sandra M. Epps of Kingstree, South Carolina; Martha Erwin, curator of the Clinchfield Railroad Museum; Ron Flanary of Big Stone Gap, Virginia; Orlis Francis of Jonesborough, Tennessee; Selena Harmon with East Tennessee State University's Archives of Appalachia; Tiffany Hemphill, records clerk for the Town of Erwin, Tennessee; Marcia Kelly with the Johnstown (Pennsylvania) Area Heritage Association; Phyllis McEwen, librarian at the Tampa-Hillsborough, Florida County Public Library; Brian Reisinger, press secretary for U.S. senator Lamar Alexander; Brenda Sparks, with the *Erwin Record*; Mike Tilley, president of the Watauga Valley Railroad Historical Society & Museum; Peggy Vignolo, administrative officer for the genealogy branch of the West Florida Public Library, Pensacola; Bob White of Erwin, Tennessee; and all the kind people who shared their photographs and stories.

Alf and Mark interviewed several people in 2014 for this book. Among them were U.S. senator and former Tennessee governor Lamar Alexander, Everette Allen, George Hatcher, Julie Kilby, Nancy Moore Pearson, Ruth Fink and Karl Thomas. Quotes attributed to those persons in this book came from those interviews, unless otherwise credited to another source.

INTRODUCTION

Whistling its way merrily through the mountains along the tracks of the 277-mile Clinchfield Railroad Company, the famed Number One, a 4-6-0-type steam locomotive built in 1882, warms the hearts of all who see and ride behind it. In a day when almost all of the beautiful steam locomotives are all but memories, here is one which, by all rights, should have long gone into a scrap pile. Yet, here it is!...A locomotive that has defied time and convention to boil water and steam mightily, giving pleasure to all who ride and watch. "Turn back, turn back, oh time in thy flight." The Number One does just that for those who ride.
—William S. "Bill" Cannon

William S. "Bill" Cannon, an associate professor of computer science and mathematics at Presbyterian College cum press representative for the Clinchfield Railroad, wrote those words more than four decades ago, summing up nicely the story of the little engine called the Clinchfield No. 1. As with most things, there are stories behind the story, and that is certainly true with the No. 1. Even its name, while singular in title, defies. It may be the Clinchfield No. 1, but men—tough, independent railroaders—lovingly call it "Rosebud."

Clinchfield railroaders doted on their little engine and were proud of its many stories—that it was born in 1882 in the heartland of America; that it was a first-on-the-scene savior for victims of the 1889 Johnstown, Pennsylvania flood (the nation's worst disaster until 9/11); that it came to the Appalachian mountains to help build a railroad; and that, despite all odds, it became a survivor and a beloved symbol of accomplishment and downright pluckiness. In *The Clinchfield No. 1: Tennessee's Legendary Steam Engine*, we aim to tell some of the little engine's stories and those of the men who shaped, saved and, yes, loved it.

Its third time out after extensive remodeling, the Clinchfield No. 1 rounds the bend at Toe River Baptist Church in Huntsdale, North Carolina, on December 7, 1968. *Photo by William S. Young.*

The locomotive was eighty-six years old before it found widespread adoration, garnering headlines in the *New York Times*, the *Washington Post*, the *Christian Science Monitor* and *Southern Living* magazine, no less, as it puffed along as the nation's oldest operating steam engine in regular service. It was rebuilt from a woebegone pile of rust and rotten wood in the autumn of 1968 and served for the next eleven years as the pride of the Clinchfield, leading excursion trains to seven state capitals; through the Appalachian mountains of Tennessee, Kentucky, Virginia and the Carolinas; over to the coast of the Atlantic Ocean; and even into downtown Tampa, Florida.

So why did the Erwin, Tennessee–based Clinchfield Railroad, which had discontinued passenger service and scrapped nearly every one of its vast fleet of steam locomotives by the mid-1950s to make room for diesels, opt to resurrect an era long gone?

There are many answers to that question, but the greatest of these may be love.

1
IN THE BEGINNING

In the towering roundhouse of the B&O Railroad Museum in Baltimore, Maryland, the Clinchfield No. 1, still shiny in silver and black, beckons visitors to come aboard. It is surrounded by much larger steam locomotives, passenger cars and assorted railroad history, but even in this special place—the birthplace of American railroading—the story of the "One Spot," as it was sometimes called, can be only partially told.

While its time on the rails ended in 1979, the No. 1's legacy lives on. It was nearly lost, twice, to the cutter's torch, but when it was born again in 1968 as a genius marketing coup by the Clinchfield Railroad, the No. 1's fame took it from the Appalachian Mountains to seven state capitals.

But we are getting ahead of ourselves.

Before the story of the Clinchfield No. 1's glory days can be told, and long before it earned the loving nickname of "Rosebud," readers must travel back more than 130 years to a railroad shop in Logansport, Indiana. That's where work on the little locomotive—if a nearly forty-two-ton machine can be called "little"—was begun on April 11, 1882. That's where this story of stories begins.

That spring day in 1882 probably wasn't an eventful beginning for the steam engine, which, at that time, was to be fitted as No. 423. It was just the building of another steam locomotive—neither the biggest nor the most elaborately designed—awaiting a life of pulling and hauling and chugging along. In fact, the *Knoxville (Tennessee) Journal* once described most of the locomotive's days as "a winding story of…hard labor on railroad tracks."

The Pennsylvania Depot in Logansport, Indiana, would have been home to steam engine 423 (the future Clinchfield No. 1). In the 1880s, this was one of the nation's busiest depots. *Courtesy of Thelma Conrad/Cass County Historical Society.*

Shopworkers in Logansport, Indiana, built steam engine 423 (future Clinchfield No. 1) in 1882. This photograph shows workers at the Logansport shops posing at the transfer table with engine No. 440. Could some of these workers have been the men who built the No. 423? Very possibly. Sadly, there is no known photograph of the engine as the 423. *Courtesy of Thelma Conrad/Cass County Historical Society.*

By mid-summer, four months after the Logansport workers had started building the engine, their work was complete, and on a hot summer's day in August 1882, No. 423 was ready to show the world what it could do. Already, the little engine was prepared to defy expectations.

The *Logansport Weekly Pharos* effusively reported the locomotive's completion in its August 16, 1882 edition: "The new freight engine, No. 423, just built at the Panhandle shops, has been given a trial, and its workings have proven first class," the newspaper wrote.

> *It easily pulled twenty loaded cars up the north hill, a job which usually requires two small locomotives. The engine is a ten-wheeler, and everything about it is constructed in the plainest and most substantial manner. It cost about $8,000. The old engine 433, whose place is supplied by this one, was purchased in 1865. It was about one-third less in size. Yet it cost $28,000. This shows that railroad machinery has dropped greatly in price within the last few years.*

Despite the obvious excitement in Logansport, fame for the engine wouldn't appear until eight decades later. As with most things, beginnings are often simple, uneventful and unremarkable. There is little doubt the workers in the Logansport railroad shops were focused on getting the next job done, perhaps creating another 4-6-0, the numbered designation for engines of the No. 1's class. When finished, the ten-wheeler weighed 83,100 pounds and had 150 pounds of boiler pressure. This G-7-class locomotive made a great workhorse. While Clinchfield Railroad documents preserved at East Tennessee State University's Archives of Appalachia indicate the No. 1 was one of several locomotives built in the Logansport shops, Evert Wolfe, a member of the Cass County (Indiana) Historical Society, said "stories conflict" on just what kind and how many engines were created there. In correspondence for this book, Wolfe wrote, "Some say this engine was the only engine built. Others say there were two or three others, but I've not been able to confirm yes or no." Likewise, Jehu Z. Powell's *History of Cass County, Indiana*, published in 1913, indicates that the primary role of the Panhandle Company's shops, operating under a roundhouse completed in May 1870, was maintenance. "The shops are large," Powell wrote, "and substantially built and fitted up with the latest machinery and they are capable of building new engines or cars, but the principal work is rebuilding and repairing the company's engines and cars." Whether

This earliest known image of the 4-6-0 engine (future Clinchfield No. 1) was taken in 1908 when operating as No. 5 for the Carolina, Clinchfield & Ohio Railroad. *Courtesy of Clinchfield Railroad Museum.*

workers built more engines at that particular shop might be lost to time, but it is clear that in August 1882, when the men finished their task at hand, the completed locomotive officially rode the tracks of the Columbus, Chicago & Indiana Central Railway. One can't help but be intrigued, though, with the notion that the Clinchfield No. 1 might be unique if it were, indeed, the one and only engine built at the Panhandle shops.

Several railroads owned the locomotive over the years, according to many sources, including James A. Goforth's excellent pictorial history book, *When Steam Ran the Clinchfield.* Still, Engine 423 was a long way, both in time and designation, from its eventual status as No. 1. The locomotive's ownership, numbers and locations have been well documented by newspaper reporters and railroad buff H. Reid in a booklet published in 1972 for the National Railway Historical Society. In *Clinchfield's Old No. 5—Now No. 1 Attraction,* Reid wrote:

In essence, the 4-6-0:

    —was completed in August 1882 at Logansport, Ind., shops as No. 423 of a Pennsylvania predecessor, the Columbia, Chicago & Indiana Railway, a 580-mile Columbus-Chicago-Indianapolis route...

    —after seven months, entered the roster of Chicago, St. Louis & Pittsburgh Railway, absorbent of CC&IC...

    —changed ownership (in 1890) to Pittsburgh, Cincinnati, Chicago & St. Louis Railway, whose stenciled identity on the tender usurped much space on its short tender. The engine number changed to 543 (in August 1899).

    —was sold in March 1900 to Ohio River & Charleston, a 34-mile line from Johnson City, Tenn., to the North Carolina border, renumbered 5 and commenced construction work on what evolved as South & Western Railway in 1902 (although some sources say 1903), and, in 1908, the Carolina, Clinchfield & Ohio and, in time (1924), simply the Clinchfield.

    —was diverted in April 1913 for a little more than $4,000 to a North Carolina short line, the Black Mountain Railway, a 25½-mile lumber and feldspar route mounted on 65-pound rail and reeling under heavy bonds subsequently made good by Clinchfield in preserving a connection with B.M. at Kona, N.C. Renumbered, again, as No. 1...

    —legally re-entered Clinchfield's holding in April 1955 prior to transfer to (town of) Erwin for proposed exhibition. Accord on suitable site never came. Nor did finalization of outright purchase by Kingsport, Tenn., businessman E.C. Bellamy.

To complete the history started by Reid, the No. 1 would be removed from the Town of Erwin's ownership and returned to the Clinchfield for rebuilding in 1968 and, finally, in 1979, for retirement to the B&O Railroad Museum in Baltimore.

The No. 1's history is part of its charm, another testament to longevity and stamina. When it was constructed as the No. 423, it was one of hundreds of steam engines in service across the nation. Reid provides a colorful description, produced with a series of the letter O, of the locomotive's ten-wheel makeup: "Appeared similar to Pennsylvania's Class E Altoona product with a firebox crammed between staggered drivers for an exaggerated Whyte definition: o o OO O."

There are no known photos of the locomotive as the No. 423 or 543. The first known image is that of the No. 5, taken in 1908 in Dante, Virginia, while on early duty for the Clinchfield. While its widespread

The engine, pictured here at its tie-up spot in Burnsville, North Carolina, was diverted in April 1913 to the Black Mountain Railway and first achieved status as No. 1. *Courtesy of the Phil Laws Collection.*

fame several decades later as the Clinchfield No. 1 was still to come, its first brush with recognition, if not fame, came only a few weeks before its seventh year—as a savior for victims of the Johnstown, Pennsylvania flood of 1889.

RELIEF TRAIN FOR THE JOHNSTOWN FLOOD OF 1889

Operating under its first numbered designation, the No. 423, the ten-wheeler was working the rails in Pittsburgh when it was called to service for one of the nation's worst disasters: the Johnstown, Pennsylvania flood, in which 2,209 people perished on May 31, 1889, after a dam failed, sending twenty million tons of water in a massive wave of destruction into the valley below.

According to an article published December 28, 1962, in the *Knoxville Journal* (nearly seventy-three years after the disaster), the No. 423 was "the first locomotive to reach Johnstown after the disastrous flood...had cut a wide swath of destruction through the Pennsylvania valley."

"But," *Journal* reporter Charles Appleton wrote,

> *to begin at the beginning: in 1851, a dam 700 feet long and 106 feet high was built across the South Fork, a branch of the Conemaugh River, at a point twelve miles above the fledgling town. Intended as a reservoir for the Pennsylvania Canal, the plans were subsequently abandoned and in 1888 the dam and surrounding properties were sold to the South Fork Hunting and Fishing Club. On May 31 of the following year at about 3:10 p.m., the center of the dam gave way after two days of continuous rain...By noon of the 31st, it had become obvious that efforts of a few members of the club to cut a new channel around the dam would be futile. The lake had reached flood level thirty minutes earlier and was continuing to rise at three feet an hour. Shortly afterward, a telegraph operator stationed at the South Fork tower of the Pennsylvania Railroad tapped out the valley's first warning*

of the impending disaster, "The dam is getting worse and may possibly go." Then, John Payne, a young civil engineer who had worked throughout the morning beside members of the hunting and fishing club, galloped on horseback through the valley shouting, "The dam can't last more than a few hours. Get to higher ground as fast as you can." Tragically, because of his youthfulness, few persons took him seriously.

When the dam broke, torrents of water swallowed the town and neighboring boroughs along the river. The Pennsylvania Railroad's stone bridge in Johnstown was not destroyed in the onslaught; rather, mounds of debris, rising twenty to thirty feet, piled up against it. The horror of the flood was manifested when survivors trapped in the tangled mess were burned alive when the debris caught fire. "The fire burned for three days and three nights," the *Journal* article said. "Firemen said it apparently ignited by live coals from either an overturned heater in some destroyed home or from an upset railroad engine's grate."

The Johnstown Area Heritage Association claims it was the single largest loss of American civilian lives in one day until the horrifying 2001 terrorist attacks on 9/11. In his 1890 book, *Through the Johnstown Flood*, the Reverend David J. Beale called the disaster "the most appalling calamity of modern times." In the preface to the book, Beale wrote:

As the sun sank behind the western foothills of the Allegheny Mountains, Wednesday evening, May the 29th, 1889, he gilded with glory the spires of a score of churches, shed his parting beams upon more than 5,000 dwellings, and lighted to their happy homes over 30,000 people in the peaceful, picturesque and industrious valley of the Conemaugh. When, on Saturday, the 1st day of June, the sun again, for the first time, looked out from behind the thick clouds, peeping over the eastern crest of the Alleghenies, he saw, indeed, the same deep valley and the same mountain peaks, but oh! how changed was Johnstown! The scene of destruction presented was unparalleled in the annals of American history, and for suddenness, destructiveness and awful horrors, perhaps, unsurpassed since the Noachian deluge. Within a few minutes, [thousands of] human beings had been launched into eternity, 2,500 homes had been utterly demolished, and property destroyed the worth of which has been estimated by millions. The businessman, the physician, the lawyer, the clergyman, the schoolteacher, the clerk, the mechanic, the laborer, the rich and the poor, the stranger and the citizen, the old and the young, parents and children, the good and the bad—all had gone down together into a common watery grave.

Within hours of the flood, members of the nation's media were scrambling to reach Johnstown, and rescue and relief efforts were being organized seventy-one miles away in Pittsburgh. The steam locomotive that would one day be known as the Clinchfield No. 1—but at this time was still the No. 423—set out with relief workers and supplies.

Nathan Daniel Shappee recounts the relief effort and the first train to set out from Pittsburgh in a doctoral thesis published in 1940 for the University of Pittsburgh. Titled "A History of Johnstown and the Great Flood of 1889: A Study of Disaster and Rehabilitation," Shappee's thesis details how the citizens of Pittsburgh were galvanized to take action for their hapless neighbors. "On June 1," Shappee wrote,

> *Pittsburgh waited impatiently for the beginning of the relief meeting at old City Hall at 1 p.m. Excited crowds had waited all night at the Union Station for information from the valley. News of the meeting had been thoroughly circulated. Newspapers had established relief funds. The chamber of commerce had organized its own committees but had abandoned them to work with the mayors' meetings. When the mayors of Pittsburgh and Allegheny arrived to take charge...the old building was packed... A "Citizens Relief Committee" was quickly formed. William McCreery was chosen chairman. James B. Scott was named chairman of a committee on railroad transportation which soon left for the railroad station to arrange for the first relief train departure.*

In an article published on June 3, 1889, in the *Pittsburgh Times*, Shappee wrote that a call for contributions to aid Johnstown was met with such enthusiasm that it was

> *impossible to keep track of the contributions...Businessmen and their employees, distillers and doctors of divinity, saloon keepers and prohibitionists, vied with each other. Differences of creed and condition disappeared in the generous rivalry of charity. There was no speech making, no oratory but the golden eloquence of cash. Big and little contributions got applause, so long as they were in proportion to the means of the giver. For almost an hour, at the rate of a thousand dollars per minute, the storm of money poured down upon the table, until $48,116.70 had been received.*

Over the next several days, donations continued to be received. "Monday morning," the *Pittsburgh Times* reported,

This stone bridge—shown several days following the disaster—captured tons of debris when the flood slammed into Johnstown. The debris caught fire, burning hapless survivors alive. *Photo from Johnstown Area Heritage Association.*

brought a veritable storm of remittances by letter and telegram while the churches and Sabbath-schools brought in their collections of pennies, silver of every denomination, bank-notes and checks, in cigar boxes, bags, papers, handkerchiefs, and in one instance, the traditional "stocking." It was an accumulation of miscellaneous collections such as no fastidious teller would take over his counter, but it held the child's penny, the widows' mites, as well as the gifts of those "that did cast in of their abundance."

The fever pitch to travel to Johnstown and render aid was so great, Shappee wrote,

that when director Scott and his party arrived at the Union Station, they had great difficulty in even getting to the passenger coach of the first relief train. Hundreds of volunteers wanted to go to the scene of the flood and the more inebriated were the most insistent. With the aid of the police, Scott finally chose seventy-five volunteers to serve as workmen. In addition to doctors, eighteen police were detailed to accompany the relief train to guard the provisions. At 4:30 p.m., the relief train left the station.

Behind the steam locomotive, "one car accommodated the men; another car was filled with coffins; while the other boxcars were filled with food, clothing, and lumber."

Appleton's *Knoxville Journal* article calls the relief train's efforts "heroic." In his article, Appleton says the locomotive

that was later to be named the Clinchfield Engine No. 1...puffed out of the Pittsburgh yards for Johnstown 78 miles to the east...In the twenty cars strung out behind the engine were the first specialists, clothing, medical supplies and food to reach the drowned town.

But what would have been a two-and-a-half-hour trip on a normal day turned into an arduous undertaking. Debris delayed the train along the way. It took until 10:00 p.m. for the train to reach Sang Hollow at the northern end of the valley, some three miles from Johnstown. "A run that should have taken between two and three hours had taken nearly twice that," Appleton wrote.

At Sang Hollow, the relief party was dismayed to see nearly four hundred feet of rails heavily damaged. En route, Scott had divided his force into two companies. Shappee wrote: "Dr. H.E. Collins was placed in charge of Company A with the understanding that he and his men would be first to proceed to Johnstown. Captain A.A. Logan was leader of Company B, which would move supplies and guard the train."

According to Shappee's account, a telegrapher informed Scott that the washout "had damaged the track until it could not support the weight of the engine. [The] work crew from Johnstown was already at work to repair the track, but several hours would pass before their repairs would be completed." But time was of the essence, so Scott's men secured two handcars and improvised a flat car to transport the goods. "Men packed goods on their backs over the hill and around the break in the track to the flat car. Trip after trip was made until two carloads of food had been carried around the break, placed on the flat car," Shappee wrote. Appleton added, "Proceeding toward Johnstown, the little group located an old work train and drove it to within about a mile of the shattered city." Shappee's thesis says these men arrived at the stone railroad bridge that had held back the debris and was still burning about 1:30 a.m. on Sunday, June 2. He wrote:

By 8 o'clock, the track had been repaired, and Scott's train went to the stone bridge. Dr. Collins has distributed his two cars of provisions while [a]waiting the daylight. The rising sun slowly gave form and distinctness to the most lurid vista upon which the tired men had ever gazed. The scene there beheld was horrible beyond description. Across the north end of the bridge, where the railroad embankment had been, swept a foul and loathsome torrent 800 feet wide. Along the east side bridge was the jagged mess of debris rising twenty feet above the tracks, crackling and smoking and filling the air with the unmistakable odor of burnt flesh. Beyond this, where Johnstown had once been was a lake, a great stretch of sandy plain and here and there clusters of partly wrecked houses. About and between these houses were piled, often fifty feet high, every form of wreckage the flood produced, locked together by hundreds of feet of wire and packed by the water into an inextricable mass. Fascinated by the scene of horror, the men stood speechless before it until their own revulsion broke their gaze.

Beale's book, too, notes that the relief train was able to complete its task that Sunday morning after "the tracks of the Pennsylvania Railroad were sufficiently repaired to permit the relief train to proceed…and considerable quantities of provisions were transferred across the Conemaugh into Johnstown proper, by means of a rope and snatch block stretched across the chasm from the end of the Conemaugh viaduct."

After giving out a few more supplies, Company B took the relief train back to Morrellville, where a depot was immediately established, Shappee wrote.

Many years later, the steam locomotive that pulled the relief train would be celebrated as a monument of railroad excellence and nostalgia, but in the days after the horrific flood, it was a beacon of hope. "The arrival of the Pittsburgh men greatly encouraged the people of the valley," Shappee wrote in his thesis, "because it made them realize that railroad communication with the outside world had again been established. In Johnstown, Kernville, Cambria City and even into Woodvale spread word of the arrival of the relief train."

BY THE NUMBERS: MORE EARLY HISTORY

The year following the Johnstown flood, the steam locomotive No. 423 came under the ownership of the Pittsburgh, Cincinnati, Chicago & St. Louis Railway, and its number changed for the next decade to the No. 543. A Clinchfield Railroad history titled *The Story of Little No. 1*, available at the Archives of Appalachia, shows the steamer's next sale came "as she aged and larger, finer locomotives were built." It was in 1900 that the engine and its tender came to Tennessee under the Ohio River and Charleston, a new railroad being pushed through the Volunteer State's mountains. At this point, its number changed from 543 to No. 5 for the Ohio River and Charleston line. Each step of the way, it got closer to its rightful place as the No. 1.

In 1902, it was included in a purchase by the South & Western Railroad, and, in 1908, by the Carolina, Clinchfield & Ohio (later simply known as the Clinchfield). *The Story of Little No. 1* details this further: "Starting a new career on the mountainous Clinchfield, [the engine] worked among the forests and coal fields until April 1913, when its owners, regarding it as an unwanted hand-me-down, leased it to a subsidiary, the Black Mountain." According to H. Reid's booklet *Clinchfield's Old No. 5—Now No. 1 Attraction*, this happened in April 1913 at a cost of "a little more than $4,000" to Black Mountain Railway, a short line with a twenty-five-and-a-half-mile lumber and feldspar route.

There it was refitted, finally, as "No. 1" and, Reid wrote, "plugged along forty years with crews pledged by Clinchfield, also providing shopping at Erwin every six months with an extensive overhaul in the

North Carolina's Black Mountain Railway, a Clinchfield Railroad subsidiary, paid $4,000 for the engine. Tennessee-based Clinchfield supplied crews and shop service every six months. *Courtesy of Martha Erwin/Clinchfield Railroad Museum.*

The Black Mountain No. 1 worked hard for four decades in North Carolina. In Burnsville, the engine replenished coal and water from this unusual square tank. *Courtesy of the Phil Laws Collection.*

The Black Mountain No. 1 was serviced at Clinchfield's Erwin, Tennessee shops. In the mid-1930s, it received an extensive overhaul, as this photo from 1936 demonstrates. *Courtesy of David Kistner Collection.*

mid-thirties." The *Georgetown Times* would later call the No. 1's years with the Black Mountain the days it was "shunted off into obscure areas to labor ingloriously in forests and coal fields" that "went on for forty-two years—no song and no salutes."

A.J. "Alf" Peoples, co-author of this book, remembers his father, Jack Peoples, an engineer for the Clinchfield Railroad, traveling to Kona, North Carolina, several times to retrieve the Black Mountain No. 1. Often called "Old Number One" even then, the locomotive was brought to Clinchfield's Erwin shops for repairs, maintenance and refurbishing. True to its name, the No. 1 was outfitted in all black and not the two-tone silver and black it would later sport following its rebuild many years later. Ken Riddle did a marvelous history of the Black Mountain No. 1 for *The Cy Crumley Scrapbook*. In it, Riddle described how the No. 1 "waddled out of Burnsville, North Carolina, to various points out in the mountains, depending on how far out in the timber the railroad was at that time." He continues:

She was small and light on her feet so she suited the little road just fine for many years. My grandpa Riddle rode the Black Mountain a few times as a boy going to his Dad's logging jobs over there, and he always commented how remarkably slow the trains went. On one occasion, he and his big brother, Tom, got off the train at a water tank and kept walking while Number 1 took water. He told me they beat the train to Burnsville by half an hour walking!

The steam engine would remain with the mountain railroad until 1955, when the Clinchfield took "the aging No. 1" back and soon sold it to the town of Erwin, Tennessee, home of the Clinchfield Railroad, for display. According to Reid, the Black Mountain No. 1's time in North Carolina ceased when the railway purchased another ten-wheeler, the Clinchfield No. 99, which was later redesignated as No. 3 before diversion as a display engine for the Casey Jones Museum in Jackson, Tennessee. Interestingly, the No. 1 and the No. 99, both used on Clinchfield's Black Mountain subsidiary, were the only two Clinchfield steam engines to escape the cutter's torch. All others were scrapped and lost to history when diesels took their place along the rails. For the Casey Jones Museum, the No. 99 was renumbered the 382. It is considered to be a close "cousin" of the No. 1.

But the No. 1's official return to Erwin and new ownership by the municipality was done with little fanfare. Clinchfield Railroad documents claim the town of Erwin took possession of the engine on December 7, 1955, but public records for the town of Erwin indicate it was actually a few weeks later. The discrepancy may come from when negotiations between the town and the railroad began. Nevertheless, the official minutes of the Erwin board of mayor and aldermen show that the purchase was approved on January 5, 1956. There seemed to be little, if any, discussion about the purchase. In fact, buying the locomotive was approved along with nearly fifty other "bills" for the town—everything from a $2.25 post office box rental fee to a $150,280.77 electric bond issue.

The price for the steam engine was $700. Alderman E.E. Woodruff made the motion to pay the bills, and it received a second from H.E. Campbell. The motion passed unanimously, with aldermen O.L. Huff and Roland McCurry also voting in favor. Alderman T.H. Peters was absent, and Mayor R.W. "Pappy" McNabb was not required to vote. The $700 was paid to the treasurer of Clinchfield's subsidiary, the Black Mountain Railway Co. Most interesting, perhaps, considering the No. 1's future fame, the purchase was listed simply as "one second-hand steam locomotive." It is often mistakenly claimed that the town of Erwin paid $1 for the engine, but it's clear that this is not the case. The buy-an-engine-for-a-buck contention does have merit,

The Black Mountain No. 1 logged nearly 200,000 miles over forty years on the short twenty-five-mile railway. John Woodruff is shown in the cab. *Photo by Dick Brown.*

The Black Mountain No. 1 was retired in 1954. The Town of Erwin bought the engine for $700. The engine unofficially became the Clinchfield No. 1. *Photo by Steve Patterson.*

but it comes many years later, when the railroad bought the engine back from the Town of Erwin. It was then, nearly thirteen years later, in 1968, that the engine changed hands once more, this time for only $1—and a promise. The September 9, 1968 minutes of the Erwin board of mayor and aldermen, recorded it thusly: "A motion was made by E.E. Woodruff and seconded by Roland McCurry that the town of Erwin enter into an agreement with the Clinchfield Railroad whereby the town will sell to the Clinchfield Railroad the Black Mountain Locomotive No. 1 for $1.00 and other considerations, providing the Clinchfield Company repairs it and puts it in use for excursion trips to accommodate the people of Erwin." The vote was unanimous with all aldermen—Woodruff, McCurry, Joe Frazier, James Peterson and Joe Hendren—voting "aye." It's interesting to note that it was alderman E.E. Woodruff who made the motion to approve the purchase in 1956 and made the motion to sell in 1968. His son, John Woodruff, is featured in a photo of the Black Mountain No. 1 in this book.

So on that September day, in Erwin's four-story municipal office building on Gay Street, and more than eighty-six years after its construction far away in Indiana, the little locomotive officially returned once more to the Clinchfield Railroad. The railroad officially took possession of the engine the following day, September 10, 1968.

4
FORLORN AND FORGOTTEN:
THE TOWN OF ERWIN YEARS

S o what happened between 1956 and 1968, from when the Town of Erwin first bought the engine to when it was returned to the railroad? In short, very little and not enough.

When the Town of Erwin bought the "second-hand steam locomotive" in the very early days of 1956, there was a chance for immortality. The plans were to remake the Black Mountain No. 1 in the image of the Clinchfield and put the little engine on display as a sign of Erwin's heritage as a railroad town. The engine would, for the first time, be known as the Clinchfield No. 1, but a little work was needed. According to an article written in 1970 by Clinchfield press representative Bill Cannon for the *Bulletin*, a National Railway Historical Society magazine, the engine "was repaired, painted, and given to…Erwin for display." By the time the town received the remodeled engine, the Black Mountain No. 1 had officially been converted to the Clinchfield No. 1. The steam engine, for the first time, had its two-tone design, with the smoke box newly painted silver in contrast with the rest of the engine's black. The words "Black Mountain" were removed from the coal tender and replaced with "Clinchfield." Where the cab had once been designated as "B.M. 1," it now had "Clinchfield 1" etched there. The wheels were trimmed in silver.

Karl Thomas, a Clinchfield carman, helped spruce up the newly dubbed Clinchfield No. 1 and its coal tender for the municipality. "When the town of Erwin took it, the underframe was all wood and a wooden deck with that steel tank sitting on top," Thomas said. "We took sheet metal and covered up that rotten wood so it wouldn't show. If we hadn't done that, that whole thing would have caved in."

The Town of Erwin planned to display the engine in a public park, but that never happened. And unfulfilled promises led to devastating consequences. *Courtesy Martha Erwin/ Clinchfield Railroad Museum.*

A new look, new paint and a new name, however, didn't lead to the expected celebration of the Clinchfield. In fact, the nearly thirteen years the locomotive remained under the care of the Town of Erwin were, without any doubt, the saddest days of the engine's long life. The engine would be shuttled about the Erwin yard, never really finding a home, as detailed in another article by Cannon, this one published in the *Western Tar Heel Civitan:* "Years passed, and it rusted behind the shops, and even had a small tree growing through its cab floor and the cab roof fell in. Things looked bad for the engine."

But it had looked promising in the beginning, especially when Erwin businessman Earle Hendren was elected alderman shortly after the town bought the engine. Hendren was in the business of entertainment. He owned three theaters in the little town of Erwin: the Lyric Theatre, the Holiday Drive-In and the Capitol Theatre, which is still in business today. For a short time, Hendren even dabbled in traveling entertainment shows. According to Lynn Abbott and Doug Seroff's book, *Ragged But Right: Black Traveling Shows, "Coon Songs," and the Dark Pathway to Blues and Jazz,* published in 2007 by the University Press of Mississippi, Hendren owned the Rabbit Foot Minstrels that included in its entertainment troupe, among other eccentricities, a "peg-legged dancer, a 268½-pound blues singer with diamonds in her teeth, and a fire eater." Hendren bought the show, which a newspaper columnist once said would be "as familiar as corn pones and black-eyed peas in some Southern towns," from F.S. Wolcott in 1950 but sold it only five years later to Eddie Moran of Monroe, Louisiana, despite getting press coverage from the *New York Times* and *Billboard* magazine, which quoted Hendren in an article on June 4, 1955, as saying the Rabbit Foot is "one of two big one-nighter colored shows left playing under canvas in the South."

Hendren was sworn into office in March 1956, only two months after the Clinchfield No. 1 officially became town property. With his background in the entertainment industry, Hendren knew putting the steam engine on display would delight children and adults alike, but the town was lackadaisical when it came to the old engine. When Hendren died unexpectedly in June 1962, the Clinchfield No. 1 lost its biggest cheerleader.

During the late 1950s, the No. 1 was given some attention while biding its time under the ownership of the Town of Erwin. The Clinchfield Railroad and the East Tennessee Chapter of the National Railway Historical Society joined together for a special railfan excursion on July 5, 1958. At a stop in Erwin, the fans were allowed to spend a few minutes exploring the No. 1, its tender and two passenger cars strung together to resemble an excursion from the past. The No. 1 and its entourage didn't head down the tracks, though, as it was purely a show-and-tell event. Still, it certainly did foreshadow what was to come a decade later, when the No. 1 would, in fact, pull its own Clinchfield excursions. In a fourth-quarter 1958 issue of the *Bulletin*, Charles K. Marsh, a longtime key railroad photographer and author of the excellent 2004 pictorial book *Clinchfield in Color*, wrote:

> *Thirty minutes after the 8 a.m. departure from Johnson City, our train was standing in Erwin while railfans clambered aboard three trains spotted for viewing. The former Black Mountain Number 1, now relettered Clinchfield, headed a two-car passenger train made up of CC&O wooden coach 123 and wooden business car 1, a Pullman product of 1906...Clinchfield Railroad officials, at first skeptical of an excursion, were very pleased at the success of the trip and have expressed interest in another in the near future.*

Even so, no one—especially a Clinchfield Railroad official—would have ever dreamed about the eleven years of excursions the No. 1 would pull from 1968 until 1979.

The engine was sold to the Clinchfield Railroad in 1968 for the bargain price of one dollar. It was noted as the purchase of "Black Mountain No. 1." *Courtesy Robert Harris Collection.*

When T.D. "Tom" Moore Jr. first saw the No. 1 in 1968, the engine—after years of neglect—was a heap of rotting wood and rusting metal. *Courtesy Bill Folsom Collection.*

Historian Jim Goforth retired from the Clinchfield Railroad as chief engineer. For many years, he had the No. 1's original faceplate in his extensive Clinchfield Railroad collection. *Courtesy Jerry Hilliard.*

Even with railfans gleefully hopping aboard the No. 1, the need for a permanent display where the public at large could view the historic engine was never found. No public park was ever created for the No. 1, so times for the little engine grew dark. In 1962, the *Knoxville Journal* wrote an apt—and stinging—criticism of its care under the Town of Erwin: "Today, the locomotive stands outside the Clinchfield Railroad Shops here, almost forgotten except for the caretakers who occasionally 'slap a coat or two of paint' on her rusting hulk."

With each passing year and no permanent home discussed, the engine, left to the elements, began to fade as its cab rotted and its boiler rusted. Photos show it resting sadly among old engines and cars ready for the scrapheap in the Erwin rail yard. Instead of a celebration of railroad history, the decaying limbo of the little engine was instead slowly becoming a testament to neglect. *The Story of Little No. 1* described the locomotive under the ownership of the town as

> *a pitiful sight…The steps and assorted other parts were falling off. The footboards were a pile of rotten wood, and the floor was gone. Termites had gorged themselves on the tender's underframe. The top half of the smoke box had rusted out. The stack was split from top to bottom. Cylinder steam chest jackets were gone. Rust had eaten large holes through the boiler coat.*

Sitting behind the Clinchfield Railroad shops, it must have looked ready, in such disrepair, for the cutter's torch.

But despite its haunted condition, the little black train wasn't yet ready for a funeral. It found a savior in 1968 in a new face at the Clinchfield Railroad: T.D. "Tom" Moore Jr., who on his second day as general manager discovered the locomotive and, like Santa Claus with a twinkle in his eye, turned to Percy "P.O." Likens, the railroad's chief mechanical officer, and asked a profound and prolific question, "Can you make that engine run?" And with those six words, Moore made Clinchfield Railroad history and began its most celebrated era.

5

THE SILVER-HAIRED MAN WITH THE MILLION-DOLLAR SMILE

Thomas D. Moore Jr., the man who saw promise in a rusting and rotting old steam engine, was a man with a vision.

As a boy, Tom Moore had walked along the railroad tracks that snaked along his family's South Carolina farm, dreaming about where those trains, pulled by puffing and powerful steam engines, could take him. But T.D. Moore Jr., as he would more commonly be known in the years ahead, wasn't just a dreamer. Born on April 8, 1917, he became a man of action and a businessman with an uncanny ability to see potential in people and properties. On those occasions when he merged his business acumen with fantastical notions of what could be, he found success where others would never have dreamed to venture.

Perhaps his unwavering devotion to the power of railroads and knowing when and how to make the right move came to Moore early in life. Its origins can be found in a story he proudly told to those closest to him, around the family's dining room table or in the back of his private railroad coach. His story would begin simply: "When I was a boy, about nine years old…"

His daughter, Nancy Moore Pearson, recalled the story she had heard many times over the years about the man she calls "her best friend."

"His father took him on a push car down the Southern Railway," Pearson said, "which was actually just across the road from the farm. And they were pushing the car. It's sort of a see-saw mechanism that powers the car, and all of a sudden, they felt the track rumble, and they both knew a train was coming." She continued:

Left: Thomas D. Moore Jr., who was also called "Tom" or "T.D.," was the eighth man appointed as Clinchfield Railroad general manager. *Photo from East Tennessee State University's Archives of Appalachia.*

Below: The Hatcher brothers have given up their spots for General Manager Moore, donning a much-in-demand white Clinchfield Railroad cap. *Courtesy Martha Erwin/Clinchfield Railroad Museum.*

And my grandfather told my father to jump, so of course he did, and he jumped out into a cotton field. But when he stood up, he was terrified because what he saw was splintered wood flying as the engine hit the push car, and all he could do is wait with bated breath as the train went by. And when it was passed, he looked across the track, and his father was waving at him with both arms, and my father ran and ran and threw his arms around him and asked, "What happened?" And my grandfather told him that he knew an old trick, but he wasn't confident enough to let my father use it, too. My grandfather told my father that the trick was to wait until the very last minute to jump. If you did, you don't get hit by the debris after you jump off because the debris goes far out beyond where you are. It seemed astonishing to me that anyone could have that kind of nerve. Those were stories that he told to his family because they involved a certain amount of faith. He was a man of faith, and he wasn't someone who wore it on his sleeve. But it was very, very important to believe that God was always with us.

The nine-year-old boy never forgot that day, and it followed him—the knowledge of when to believe and when to take a leap of faith—for much of his career as a railroad man. He was born in the community of White Oak, South Carolina, just outside the city of Winnsboro, about thirty miles from Columbia. Nostalgia for his birthplace stayed with him all his life, and White Oak is where he would return to spend the last years of his life.

During his eleven-year career as general manager of the Clinchfield Railroad and overseeing the excursions for the Clinchfield No. 1, Moore had the best passenger car, one with air conditioning and reclining seats, renamed the White Oak. Passengers paid extra to travel in it. "His heart was always in White Oak," Pearson said, "no matter where we lived. He had that wonderful rural upbringing that stayed with him all his life."

When Moore was named general manager of the Clinchfield Railroad, he brought his family from Jacksonville, Florida, to Erwin, Tennessee, the headquarters of the 277-mile railroad that stretched from Elkhorn City, Kentucky, to Spartanburg, South Carolina. "We lived all over the Southeast as he worked his way up through the ranks of railroad management, moving every one to three years, basically," Pearson recalled, noting she was a junior in high school when her family came to Erwin. She continued:

We had moved many times, so the move itself was not a shock. Moving from Jacksonville to Erwin was sort of an event, I guess, because

Jacksonville was a rather metropolitan city where I had gone to a private school. And Erwin is a small town in a beautiful, gorgeous setting…Erwin was a wonderful place to be and so different from any place I had been. It was right in the middle of the mountains with such a wonderful setting with the Nolichucky River, where kids went rafting and jumped out of platforms and trees and did all kinds of reckless things. My dad and I had always managed to have a horse or two from the time I was about twelve or so. In Erwin, we got to keep the horse fairly close by, and we both got to ride frequently on weekends, which was great. We didn't have to drive an hour to get to the animals…We lived on Spruce Street, an area known as Snob Hill.

Before he started his railroad career and went to work for the Southern Railway, Moore taught history for three years, but his father was a railroad man, so a life on the rails—or, at least, the business of railroads—drew him away from academia.

Bill Cannon once wrote about his friend's early career: "One day he got a letter from his father stating that the Southern was seeking 'Rodmen' on their survey teams out of Charlotte, and here was the chance to break into railroading, which had always been a dream of Tom's," Cannon recalled. "Tom had worked with his father's section gang between his junior and senior year, so he had some experience. He applied for and got the job in Charlotte, beginning work there on June 1, 1943. Tom tells a story of being sent on assignment to Alexandria, and since it was wartime, he could get no space, coach or sleep, to return to Charlotte—so he slept atop a coffin in the baggage car." Later, Moore moved from the engineering department to become an apprentice track supervisor, "just what he wanted so as to 'be like father.' "

"I always wanted to work on the railroads. It seemed such an important industry to me," Moore said in a March 1973 cover story in *Trains* magazine titled "Tom's Engine."

"My father rode the rails at his daddy's knees," his daughter said. "He is one of the few people I have ever known who absolutely got up every morning raring to go to work. He couldn't possibly have done anything else. He was offered jobs in other industries, and he could have probably made far more money, but that wasn't who he was. He was a railroad man. He wasn't just a businessman. He was an operations man. He knew what was going on in all phases of the business. Even when he was general manager, he went out to derailments in the middle of the night, which was virtually unheard of, I think, because he wanted to know what was happening. He wanted to see that the people who were working the derailment, to clear it, were properly fed and housed. He told me once that he made sure they got the best food he could find because he knew if they were taken care of and not hungry, if they were satisfied, that they would do a better job and be safer. He just loved his work."

And loving his work meant that family time was also railroad time. "That was dinner table conversation," Pearson said.

> *Railroad stories were something I grew up with; if we weren't talking about politics or religion, those other two things you're not supposed to talk about at the table, but we did anyway, of course. My father couldn't leave the railroad at the office because it consumed him. But we were curious…about what his day was like. I remember one particular derailment, he was called out on in the middle of the night, that had happened on some mountain path, out of Erwin. He said when he arrived, everyone was hustling, and I imagine even more so when he got there, but some very peculiar things happened. There were a number of large boulders that had been dislodged during the accident. One of the boulders, which he described as being the size of our dining room table, fell from a good height and landed right at his feet, and he said just a few minutes later, the derrick they were using to move the cars had a big piece of rail that it was moving away from the track, and the derrick dropped the rail, and he said he felt it in the air as it literally whizzed right past his ear. And he said he began to wonder, as a railroad man—and all railroaders are superstitious to some extent—that bad things happen in threes. He wondered if he shouldn't leave before the third thing happened. I was thinking, "Daddy, you need to take care of yourself!"*

His daughter needn't have worried, for Moore knew how to handle himself on the railroad. His long and winding career had taught him well. After his first job in the engineering department, Moore would work in eleven cities in seven states for four railroads as a trainmaster, superintendent, general industrial agent and assistant vice-president. "Transfer followed transfer," Cannon wrote, "with Moore meeting people and learning the layout and operations of the system…It all worked out and led to promotion after promotion" before his last career job brought him to the Clinchfield in 1968 as general manager and, in 1976, executive vice-president.

"He took over the Clinchfield," Cannon summarized, "made several operating changes, found and restored steamer Number One, got excursion

Impeccably dressed, General Manager Moore poses at the Erwin train station with his famous little steam engine in April 1972. *Courtesy of the P.O. Likens Collection.*

cars for it, and as has been said, made lots of folks happy showing them this fabulous mountain railroad and its scenery."

On the job, Moore commanded respect, not just as the boss, but also in his appearance. He stood at five feet, nine and a half inches, but broad shoulders, a good posture and always sporting a summertime tan made him appear taller. *Sandlapper* magazine described him as a "handsome, silver-haired" gentleman "beaming with quiet pride," whereas William S. Young's *Railroading* magazine described him as "a cheerful man with prominent eyebrows." He had dark green eyes, coupled with a smile politicians would pay good money to have. "A friend of mine told him once that he had a million-dollar smile, and he did; and he smiled a lot," Pearson said. "He could light up a room…The million-dollar smile never left him, never did, never did."

Moore's office in the three-story Clinchfield headquarters in Erwin couldn't compare to Car 100, his private car and rolling office. Weighing an astonishing 104 tons, the car consisted of an office with two telephone lines, three bedrooms, a kitchen and a formal dining room. When included on the Clinchfield No. 1's excursions or any other time on the rail, an invitation to Car 100 would have been considered quite an honor. But to his daughter, it was simply a workplace. "If railroading is your business or is your father's business, you just assume that everybody just views it as an everyday sort of thing," she said.

> *It never seemed to me to be a special thing that there was this office car, which everybody else called a private car, but we always called it an office car because that's what it was, his office on wheels. He was generally in the living room area, facing backward, so that he could look at the track as the train was moving and making sure everything was in order. So the whole business of riding on a train never seemed very romantic to me until the steam engine came along, and then that was a whole new ball of wax. People loved, just loved, being on the train.*

Having the No. 1 rebuilt and finding success, both in the number of excursion passengers and the good publicity it brought the railroad, as well as overseeing the controversial but immensely successful building of the "High Line" from Johnson City, stand out as two of Moore's most public success stories as Clinchfield general manager. "Without a doubt, general manager T.D. Moore was the initiator, sponsor and godfather of the surprising excursion program," Charles K. Marsh wrote in *Clinchfield in Color* and called the successful excursions "a public relations coup" for Moore. He added, "Although opposed by many in [Seaboard Coast Line] management, Moore saw the excursion trains as a wonderful way to increase the railroad's positive image at a relatively small cost. Then, too, he simply enjoyed the publicity."

His daughter, though, doesn't think personal PR was a main motivator for her father. "He was very goal oriented," she said.

> *I'm sure he was realistic enough that it could be done, but once he had his own experts say the engineering was feasible and that it could be accomplished if things were done the right way, then he wouldn't listen to*

naysayers…The Clinchfield was more than excursions and the No. 1. It was a complicated, profitable, tough sort of business. Railroading is very much like the army, I would imagine in many ways. It requires discipline, energy and planning, and so the restoration of the No. 1 and the excursions was the icing on the cake. What went on behind the scenes was much more difficult than most people would have imagined just looking at this romantic, nostalgic, beautiful steam engine. There was some pretty grueling work that supported all of this. I am so proud of the fact that my father wasn't just a dreamer. I am so proud of the fact that he also made the railroad run, and run at a profit, which enabled employees to support their families and to send their children to college. My father was a very practical man, a man who got things done but who never forgot where he came from or where he got his ability to accomplish these things. He was kind and loving and also resilient and tough. He was as loyal to his employees as I think they were to him, and that makes me very, very proud.

One of those employees, Everette Allen, remembered Moore as "determined." "If he set his mind to do something, he did it," Allen said.

I just really, really appreciated Mr. Moore. He was really good to me. If you didn't do a good job, he didn't hesitate to tell you, either. He used stern words, but he always rewarded for a good job. I don't have nothing negative to say about him. If I had to characterize Mr. Moore, I would do it with one word. He was a railroader. That one word sums him up, because he knew the railroad. He knew what it took to be a railroad man. And he loved the railroad. Anyone who knew him, no matter what else they may think about him, if they're being honest, they'd have to say that about him.

Moore himself admitted to Bob Boyd, staff writer with the *Charlotte Observer* in 1971, that he "was sort of a rare breed." "I'm an operating [administrative] man," he said, "and, as a rule, operating men don't like to fool with [passenger service] because there's no money in it." But even then, Moore was being evasive. The railroad did make money off the excursions, certainly more than passenger service of old had done in the end, and the publicity alone was priceless.

The Hatcher brothers, Ed and George, were hand-picked by Moore as engineer and fireman and unofficial spokesmen to ensure the Clinchfield No. 1 lived up to his vision. The confidence he had in them was repaid

As engineer Ed Hatcher looks on, Clinchfield general manager T.D. "Tom" Moore took the first turn at the throttle for Clinchfield No. 1's inaugural run. *Courtesy of the Nancy Moore Pearson Collection.*

with unabashed devotion. "Mr. Moore was a hard man to work for, but people were loyal to him," George Hatcher said. "He appreciated people who wanted to do a good job. If you did a good job for Mr. Moore, he'd pat on you on the back and tell you so. He could tell if you cared about the job you did." But the railfan from childhood didn't always wear his businessman persona, Hatcher said, noting that Moore "was a different man riding the One Spot. He was like a kid with a new toy." He took the Clinchfield's revitalized passenger service to heart and wanted to make sure it succeeded. "He enjoyed people and seeing people enjoy it," Hatcher said. "I think when we went on these excursions, and he saw the people enjoying it, it gave him great pleasure. It put a smile on his face."

And Pearson admits, too, that she is "a biased observer." "He was my best friend as long as he lived," she said. "He had a great sense of humor and loved to tell stories, and I think his best feature was, he was a wonderful listener…He made you feel like you were the only person in the room."

Cannon may have worked as Moore's go-to publicity man, but the two also became good friends. "He never, in all our years together," he wrote, "spoke a harsh word to me, but he would let out to me as a 'sounding board' about others who had him peeved at the moment. He was not an unreasonable man, but he simply wanted things done his way and promptly. He could see things clearly from an operating viewpoint...Thomas D. Moore Jr. was a good railroader, a kind and understanding man and an even greater friend."

In 1971, *Sandlapper* magazine noted that Moore liked to talk about the farm where he grew up as much as the railroad. The interviewer, Edward B. Borden, asked when the time came to retire back to the farm if Moore would "put a steam-driven locomotive on it." With a sly wink, Moore said, "You can never tell. I just might."

He never had a locomotive in retirement, his daughter said, but he did have a caboose. Moore died in South Carolina on July 22, 1989. He was seventy-two and the undoubted savior of the Clinchfield No. 1, whose fame and adoration would never have happened had it not been for Moore's vision.

6

REBUILDING, REMODELING AND THE TRUE MAKING OF THE CLINCHFIELD NO. 1

T.D. Moore Jr., the just-on-the-job general manager, had asked the question, "Can you make that engine run?" and P.O. Likens, as the good chief mechanical officer he was, had answered in the affirmative but with the caveat, "It may take a little money, a lot of work and time to beg, buy and make parts." And according to H. Reid, Moore's immediate reply was: "Do it."

Likens, a longtime railroader with expert knowledge of steam engines, was the take-charge man for the job. He's credited with drawing up a diagram for the locomotive's rebuild, complete with height and width measurements for everything from the wheels to the boiler to the cab. Moore recognized the monumental task he was asking of Likens and his team of workers. In 1971, he told *Sandlapper* magazine, "It was so rusted the cab was almost gone. A tree had grown up between the tank and the main body…I knew what I was going to do with it the minute I saw it. I was going to put Old No. 1 back on the line." To do so meant a change in company policy, as the Clinchfield's steam engines had more or less been retired in 1953, with passenger service being discontinued two years later in 1955. The decision to stop passenger service came about over several months and coincided with the decline of the steam locomotive, a disappointing fact to many who loved to ride the rails along one of the most beautiful routes in the nation. In a March 3, 1954 letter to Clinchfield superintendent D.H. Hendrix, R.M. Emery of Port Jefferson, New York, wrote, "I hate to bother you with such trivial matters, but two other fellows and myself are planning a trip on your line in April on train #37 or 38 over the entire line. Now what we all want

In September 1968, Clinchfield workers started the rebuild with a rusted and rotten eighty-six-year-old steam engine that had miraculously escaped the cutter's torch. *Courtesy of the Nancy Moore Pearson Collection.*

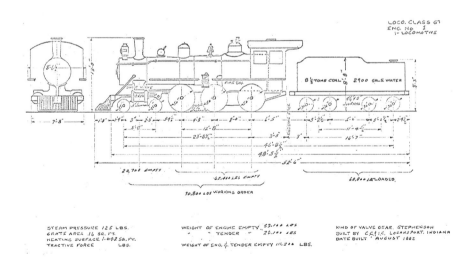

Clinchfield Railroad chief mechanical officer P.O. Likens has been credited with this hand-drawn sketch and specifications for the "new" Clinchfield No. 1. *Courtesy of Martha Erwin and the Clinchfield Railroad Museum.*

to know is this: Is #37 and 38 still hauled by a steam engine or not? That's all we want to find out, whether it's steam or not." Superintendent Hendrix replied, "In answer to your question, we are now using a diesel locomotive on trains Nos. 37 and 38. We have twelve steam locomotives in service on the Clinchfield at this time, and they are used only in case of emergency. Our present plans call for complete dieselization by end of this year." Mr. Emery and his friends, it seems, were too late and too early, as passenger and steam service were winding down in 1954 and they were nearly fourteen years away from Moore's daring plan to return both steam and passenger service to the Clinchfield.

A story about Moore in Erskine College's alumni magazine noted that the railroad's board of directors approved $9,500 for the restoration of the Clinchfield No. 1. Work began on No. 1's metamorphosis on September 23, 1968, just thirteen days after the railroad paid $1 to the Town of Erwin and officially took back the engine from the municipality.

"So followed an extensive overhaul," wrote Bill Cannon in his role as the Clinchfield's press representative. "After all, the last steamer had long ago been overhauled in the big shops. But the skills were still in Erwin, and everybody wanted to help." Not that it was easy. First "was the routing of a nest of yellow jackets from No. 1's innards," *Railroading* magazine detailed in 1969, and then there was the sting that the "engine was a mess," as Likens told Brooks Pepper, columnist for the *West Virginia Hillbilly* newspaper in August 1969. "We retubed it, replaced the pilot, cab, stack and tender underframe, installed a lubrication system, had the drivers turned—the men really worked hard on that engine," Likens said, "but they enjoyed it. We got it out of the shop in time for the Santa Claus special in November, and it's been on the go ever since."

H. Reid's booklet provides a list of Likens's early accomplishments with the rebuild, assisted by nearly four dozen Clinchfield workers, some on the clock, some on the job simply because they loved the idea of restoring steam to prominence:

> *Gentlemanly Likens:*
>   – *first chopped down a sapling growing between cab and tender.*
>   – *resisted temptation in fabricating a false, period headlamp.*
>   – *re-ringed bronzed up pistons.*
>   – *hung an old Clinchfield 2-8-2 bell in No. 1's bracket.*
>   – *refurbished crosshead guides.*
>   – *added lubricator pads for engine truck brasses.*

— reworked smokebox and stack.
— installed new and larger, pinched-end tubes.
— sawed a bridge timber into a new pilot beam.
— cut in more bridge wood for tender underframing.
— fashioned new pump rings.
— relagged boiler and applied jacket sheeting iron located in Chicago.
— replaced injectors.
— smoothed up blind drivers.
— and found other tires along with staybolts in good order.

In a press release distributed many years later by the Family Lines System, the railroad recounted how the rebuild was initially fraught with problems: "Few, if any, manufacturers stocked parts for old steam locomotives, so Likens and his shop forces improvised...Gauges and other cab appliances were bought new or found in operating condition elsewhere. Lack of a lubricator almost ended the project, until Likens located one in a Marion, North Carolina, machine shop. The owner traded it for a locomotive ride!"

The best description of the project was recalled in *The Story of Little No. 1*, in which Likens's task is likened to a "challenging game." It continues:

Draftsmen and machinists spent many days turning out drawings, blue prints and patterns. Shopmen quickly warmed to the task and generated a special pride in restoring the little ten-wheeler to regular service...Carpenters made wooden parts from bridge timbers. Sheet metal craftsmen rolled and forged new creations. A Chicago fabricator provided boiler jacketing. A new number plate was re-tooled from an old steam locomotive part someone found lying around. Shopmen turned and re-grooved piston heads. Air-actuated sanders replaced the original hand models. All appliances and gauges in the cab had to be bought new or found in operating condition elsewhere.

Karl Thomas drew up the plans to rebuild the engine's wooden cab. In a 2014 interview, the eighty-five-year-old retired carman said, "I came in to work one morning, and Mr. Likens was sitting in the office. He called me in and said, 'Tomorrow morning when you come in, I want you to bring your drawing equipment.' And I said, 'For what?' Well, he told me, 'We're going to rebuild the No. 1, and I want you to draw a set of plans for the cab.'"

For the next three days, Thomas, who had been employed by the railroad since March 23, 1950, worked on the plans, which he described as

Once inside the shops, the No. 1 became a shell of its former self as nearly four dozen workers began rebuilding the steam engine. *Courtesy of the Nancy Moore Pearson Collection.*

not being "very detailed" but more of a "rough drawing of the cab's size." He had taken some drafting classes in hopes of being an architect before opting instead for a railroad career, and Likens knew this, which Thomas guessed is why he was assigned to draw the new cab's specifications. "The wood was fairly rotten on the cab before we set out to rebuild it," he said. He continues:

> *It was in really bad shape. And beyond the cab, the smoke stack was cracked all the way from the top to the bottom. On the rebuilding, I started working on the coal tender's underframe. I remember the center of the tender was made from a bridge timber. It was originally made from wood, but all we could find to rework was a twelve-by-fourteen bridge timber. More or less, we had to figure things out like that. The pilot beam—the part that goes across the front and attaches to the cow-catcher—on the engine was also a piece of bridge timber. I remember Willard Shelton and T.J. Runion cut it with a cross-cut saw. I think some of the old-timers volunteered, but the wood part was all done by the carmen on the clock.*

Herbert Phillips and Roscoe Higgins peer over the No. 1's wheels, temporarily removed from underneath its body, which hangs above Raymond Morris and R. Peterson. *Courtesy of the Nancy Moore Peterson Collection.*

John Jones, who served as the rebuilding project's boilermaker, rolls the Clinchfield No. 1's newly installed flues. *Courtesy of the Nancy Moore Pearson Collection.*

And according to a March 1973 *Trains* magazine article, "the headlight and dynamo were overhauled," and a new number plate for the smokebox was tooled from a piece of brass taken from a retired steam E-class Challenger.

George Hatcher, the No. 1's famous fireman, said many Clinchfield workers did, in fact, volunteer during the remodel. Like the North Carolina machine shop owner who provided the needed lubricator, the volunteers (and those on payroll, too) were promised a trip back in time behind the steam locomotive once it was back on the rails. "T.D. Moore told them if they would come down and work, he'd give them a ride to Elkhorn, Kentucky. And they did, and he kept his word," Hatcher said.

> *Those men would have done it a dozen times to get to do that...The people who worked on rebuilding the No. 1, it was personal to those men. They'd come down on their day off and work...for nothing...They had a lot of pride for the steam engine, and the No. 1 gave those men something to be proud of. It couldn't have been done if they didn't do it. They did it for love of the railroad.*

Nearly four dozen men are credited with rebuilding No. 1, but there may have been railroaders who aided fellow workers in small, uncredited tasks. T.D. Moore Jr. and P.O. Likens are rightfully credited with saving the Clinchfield No. 1, as they put the remodeling project in motion, but it was the Clinchfield railroad workers who did the hands-on work. A list of those workers, however, was never officially compiled until 2013, when, using retired workers as sources, the names of the men were included in the book *The One & Only: A Pictorial History of the Clinchfield No. 1*. Machinists were Raymond Bailey, Earl Bennett, Larry Briggs, John "Kyle" Cacy, Briscoe Deaton, Orlis Francis, Oscar Grindstaff, Ted Harrison, John Hart, Harry Shell, George Street and Earle Walker. Pipefitters were Tom Ford, Claude Richardson and Russell Tittle. Painters were Gene Miller and H.C. Rogers. Electricians were Clifford Gilbert, R.C. Gilbert, K.L. Kerns and Herb Phillips. Boilermakers were Robert R. Duns, Paul Garland, John Jones, O.L. Shell and Everett Dick Tinker. Laborers were Jim Adams, E.C. Watson and Arnold Webb. The blacksmith was Buster Hughes. Carmen were Floyd Buck, Lawrence Cash, R.C. Edwards, Reed Erwin, Charlie Fowler, Ralph Hampton, James McNabb, R. Peterson, Willard Shelton, Karl Thomas and Wayne Tipton. Foremen were Harley Allen, Jack Britt, Malone Peterson and Karl Thomas.

Machinist John "Kyle" Cacy is credited as P.O. Likens's go-to man for the project and was considered the pilot of the rebuilding team. Cacy died in 1983, but his sister, Ruth Fink, remembers her brother as a dedicated toolmaker for the railroad. "One time, he took his daughter to work with him because he didn't have anyone to keep her," Fink said. "He set her up on a toolbox while he worked. His job was the love of his life. He grew up with the railroad. He was born into it."

Remarkably, the restoration project took less than two months to complete. In fact, on November 14, the steam locomotive was being shuttled between the repair shop and the paint shop, followed four days later, on November 18, by Likens, at 10:40 a.m. striking a match "to light the first fire she had felt in nearly fifteen and a half years," according to *Railroading* magazine. The local newspaper, the *Erwin Record*, wrote, "The Clinchfield Railroad No. 1 is running again. The little engine was out for yard trials Monday as railroad VIPs saw the little engine in running condition for the first time in years."

Perhaps the best description comes from original railroad documents: "When it was all together, No. 1 was a splendid thing to behold. Copper sheathing, polished to a mirror finish, enclosed the sand and steam domes. The smokestack looked out from behind a coat of gleaming white (silver).

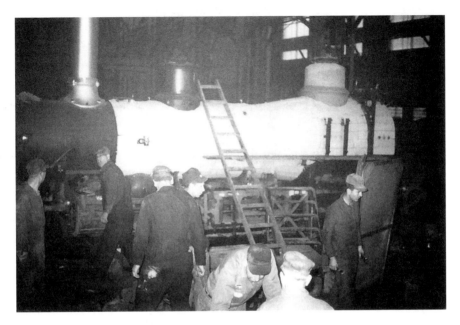

Workers (from left) Pete Mauk, Tom Ford, Dick Tinker, Lawrence Shell, Claude Richardson, unidentified and Earl Bennett add insulation to the No. 1's boiler. *Courtesy of the Nancy Moore Pearson Collection.*

A dusting of snow had fallen in Erwin on November 14, 1968, when the No. 1 was moved from the back shop to the paint shop. *Courtesy of the David Kistner Collection.*

Left: The Clinchfield No. 1 got a new faceplate and much larger "1," leaving no doubt as to her much-vaunted position as the railroad's shining star. *Courtesy of the Nancy Moore Pearson Collection.*

Below: On Love Hill, in Erwin, for the first photo shoot as the "new" Clinchfield No. 1 prior to her November 23, 1968 shakedown trip. *Courtesy of the Nancy Moore Pearson Collection.*

Silver paint covered the locomotive tires. (Yes, locomotives ride on tires, but they are made of steel.) Gold trim, artistically applied, made the locomotive a machine of unbelievable beauty and splendor." *Hillbilly* columnist Pepper called it "a sight to stir the blood! Bright and brave," he wrote, "in glossy black paint, graphited smokebox, gilt lettering and a touch of frivolity in the copper bands on sandbox, dome and air pump, the engine was, and is, a fine example of restrained good taste in restoration."

After the work had been completed, and every piece and part molded, fired, twisted and turned, the biggest test was yet to come. The remodeled No. 1 had to be able to ride the rails and pull a train.

H. Reid described it like this: "In early November 1968, Ed and George (Hatcher) cautiously shunted No. 1 in the yards behind the general office to an elegant gallery, a pittance pitted against standing-room-only crowds days later and ever since out on the main." A shakedown trip was set for November 23. On that initial outing, Reid noted that Likens fired up No. 1 for "a trial trek to Kingsport. Moore took a turn at the throttle." In tow were two coaches and Moore's personal business car, No. 100, itself weighing 104 tons after being adapted from a Coast Line diner. The tonnage behind the No. 1 strained the locomotive and "Ed's spine," Reid noted, adding, "Moreover, a brass ran hot and had to be mended before the 26th annual Santa Claus train would jingle-bell through the avenue of Appalachia austerity." The Clinchfield Railroad had been running the Santa Train through Kentucky, Virginia and Tennessee since 1942, delivering presents to excited mountain children along the rails. Moore wanted his shining new star to lead the way in 1968, and he had only days to make sure the No. 1 was up to the task. But on that trial run from Erwin, the train traveled through the town of Unicoi, into Johnson City and, finally, to Kingsport and back again.

Moore was jubilant, and he blew the train's revamped whistle for the first time—a task, and honor, he insisted be his. After that day, though, running the train—and blowing that soon-to-be iconic whistle—fell to two men: the Hatcher brothers, Ed and George.

7

THE HATCHER BROTHERS

E d runs. George fires.

That's as succinctly as H. Reid could make his apt description of the Hatcher brothers, who became as synonymous with Clinchfield Railroad history as the iconic steam locomotive the two powered through the South for eleven years. Ed and George were the sons of Fanny Lasure Hatcher and George L. Hatcher Sr., a Clinchfield Railroad conductor. The brothers had nine other siblings and grew up in a large home in the Canah Chapel community of Erwin. Ed was born on January 27, 1917, and George on October 14, 1920, which, he likes to point out, is also the birthdate of General Dwight D. Eisenhower.

Ed was confident and a star athlete at Unicoi County's only high school. He went on to play for East Tennessee State College in nearby Johnson City, where he became an All-American fullback on the football team. He was easy-going and employed a dry sense of humor. Like his older brother, George was a good athlete, known for many years, even late in life, as a star runner and bicyclist. Growing up, the brothers were inseparable, so it surprised no one to see them working side by side on the railroad.

Ed went to work for the railroad on January 25, 1940, and George signed on for railroad work on December 7, 1941, the day the Japanese attacked Pearl Harbor. George reported for railroad work the next day, but a little more than six months later, he enlisted in the war effort with the U.S. Army Air Corps on June 25, 1942. On January 9, 1943, he left to serve in the war. Soon after, Ed left his railroad job behind and also signed up to fight in the War to End All Wars.

Brothers Ed and George Hatcher were handpicked by General Manager Moore to take charge of his revamped steam locomotive—Ed for engineer and George for fireman. *Photo by Roger Cook.*

Before George became a household name as the No. 1's exuberant fireman, he made Erwin history in another way: as a German prisoner of war and a member of what would become known as "the Erwin Nine." Nine young men from the small town of Erwin, population 3,350, had all

Ed Hatcher at the throttle inside the Clinchfield No. 1's cab. Not only could he guide the Clinchfield No. 1 there, but also a specially designed device gave him control of any diesels working behind the No. 1 for added push. *Courtesy of the Russell Moore Collection.*

With his charming demeanor, George Hatcher was at ease with passengers, all of whom wanted to have a chat and maybe even nab an autograph. *Photo by Roger Cook.*

volunteered to serve in the U.S. Army Air Corps. None served together, and all were shot down at different times and in different locations. Amazingly, though, despite there being more than fifty prison camps throughout Nazi Germany, all nine Erwin men were captured and sent to the same POW camp, Stalag Luft IV. Their stories are told in Hilda Padgett's excellent volume, *The Erwin Nine*, and in George's own thirty-eight-page book, titled simply *My World War II Experiences*. After he and his fellow prisoners were liberated by the Fourteenth Armored Division of the Third Army, George returned to work for the railroad on October 22, 1945, followed soon after by Ed. Both had survived the war and were eager to return to a familiar life in Erwin.

Ed and George both served as engineers on freight trains for the Clinchfield. Both had run steam engines, but by 1968, when the No. 1 was overhauled, they, like all their co-workers, were operating diesels. With nearly fifty years' experience between them, the brothers were just what general manager T.D. Moore was looking for in a team to run his prized steam locomotive. He also wanted loyal men who would embrace the job with a passion and a duty, and the men needed to be strong and have the stamina to do the hard work. The restoration of the No. 1 was already under way when Robert Rice, assistant road foreman, called George at his home and asked if he could come down to see Moore. When George arrived, the general manager asked him straight out: "Will you be the fireman for No. 1?" "Well," George recalled in a 2014 interview for this book,

> the first thing I said was, "Who's going to run it?" And Mr. Moore said, "Your big brother." I told him I'd only fire her for Ed Hatcher and no one else. I had a regular job and made it clear that I was not to be called for anybody else...Ed Hatcher was a good engineer. He could run them like nobody else. I would know what he was going to do, and he knew what I was going to do.

Over the years, the brothers, immediately popular with the media, enjoyed playing down their skills and playing up tall tales. A couple of examples:

Ed said to *Sandlapper* magazine in 1971: "We got this job because we scored lowest on the engineer's exam."

George told Dot Jackson, columnist for the *Charlotte Observer*, in 1972: "Well, they got 90 engineers workin' for the Clinchfield. When they started runnin' this thing again, why they had us all draw straws t'see who'd have to do it. Ed drew the shortest 'un and I drew the next shortest."

The Hatchers actually took immense pride in being the driving force behind the No. 1. "The truth is," Moore once said, "the Hatchers don't like anyone else touching No. 1. They love that old engine." Brooks Pepper, the *West Virginia Hillbilly* columnist, wrote in 1969:

> *A description of the One Spot, its train and its railroad, would be incomplete without mention of its crew, the brothers Ed and George Hatcher. The Hatchers have been in the cab of the old engine on nearly every one of its trips, Ed at the throttle and George at the coal scoop. Both men are engineers of some years' standing, and both have regular runs. From the careful attention the brothers give the engine and the skill with which they run and fire it, it is evident that they are genuinely fond of it. The One Spot returns the care by not breaking down.*

Bill Cannon once wrote that Ed Hatcher "pampers and pets the Number One with plenty of tender loving care."

His first time aboard the No. 1 was a learning experience for George, who remembers that he "had to use a lot of muscle to open the throttle. I had to learn how to fire the engine," he said.

> *You might not believe this, but when you shovel coal, the fire box lights up so you can't see nothing but white hot. So I had to learn to count the scoops of coals to know where to put them. I put nine scoops of coal. That way, I had a level fire…Each and every steam engine has a different personality. A diesel is clean and very efficient, but, for some reason, we had all fallen in love with the steam engine. I was honored to be offered to fire the One Spot. My seniority really shouldn't have let me fire a steam engine, but I jumped at the chance.*

The brothers were instant celebrities, and the passengers wanted to hear the No. 1's whistle pierce the mountains and bounce through the valleys. In his marvelous book *Trains, Trestles & Tunnels: Railroads of the Southern Appalachians*, Lou Harshaw wrote, "What great charisma the two Hatchers have! Their coveralls were immaculate, pressed knife sharp, and their handsome ruggedness portrayed perfect images of the railroad folk heroes of the earlier days."

The Hatchers were the perfect men for the job, and they took their roles seriously. "A lot of people would want to talk to us, have our autographs and talk about the engine," George said,

The Hatcher brothers made sure the No. 1 received everything it needed to stay in shape. Here, after an excursion to St. Paul, Virginia, Ed offers some oil. *Photo by Roger Cook.*

and they'd get in the cab and want to know what makes it go and how do you fire it. And, you know what? It never got old. I was proud to work on a steam engine. I was proud to work on the No. 1. I welcomed the people asking questions. I'd let people ride it for a little while. I asked Mr. Moore about that once. I said, "I know I'm not supposed to, but once in a while if

George Hatcher applies a little window cleaner to the cab's glass on a June 8, 1974 stop in Spruce Pine, North Carolina. *Photo by Roger Cook.*

there's a special reason, can I do it?" He said, "Now, George, I don't want anyone getting hurt, but, OK, go ahead."

One of those passengers was nine-year-old Julie Kilby, daughter of Tom Jennings, the Clinchfield's road foreman for engines. "I kind of grew up riding the No. 1 Spot," Kilby recalled.

I was very fortunate to get to know George and Ed Hatcher and all the guys on the train, and one of the things I was very fortunate to do was ride the engine itself…I had always seen…how beautiful it was…I just remember feeling the heat from where they'd been putting the coal in. It was very scary, because the first thing George said to me was, "Be careful, Julie, don't get near it because it gets very hot and can burn you." It was almost a different respect for it, because you could feel the power of it. They let me do the horn, and there was a certain whistle it would do. I had the whistle remembered, and it would go, "Doo, Dooooo, Do, Do." So I tried to do the whistle like that…It was almost like a rope-like handle that swung down. I had to reach up kind of high for it, really, and I was standing in the seat with Ed holding me. I just remember trying to pull it down, and I thought it would be so easy, but the steam coming from just the whistle, it was hard for me to do. I had to…get my knees up and really pull with two hands. It totally took me back, because I thought it would be so light and not hard to do at all…Even the way that they had their signature whistle, it was hard to do. Again, a lot of respect for what they did and how they did it. Those guys worked hard. I loved George and Ed…I can still smell the coal burning, and to me, it's like a childhood memory for me—like warm cookies baking might be for someone else.

Wherever the Hatchers guided the No. 1, the people always came, sometimes flocking in large numbers to greet it or, at other times, a small family waiting by the railroad tracks or sometimes just a wide-eyed boy waving as the train passed. "The people," Ed told *Sandlapper* magazine in 1971, "come a-flocking. Somehow steam-driven locomotives always did that. Diesels never have."

When interviewed for this book, George hadn't seen the No. 1 in nearly thirty-five years, but the memories were still vivid. When asked if it was an honor to have senators, governors and celebrities aboard, as the train often did, George quickly said,

It was an honor to haul whoever was on board. It was such an exciting time for the people who had a chance to ride. It was an honor that people wanted to ask me questions. People would ask Ed questions, too, but he usually would say, "Ask George." It was our livelihood and our honor. Ed Hatcher had a way about him. Everybody loved him. Ed was well liked by everybody and had a wonderful sense of humor. He'd make you laugh about everything.

Ed died only a few months after the railroad retired the No. 1 in 1979.

"Ed and I knew that steam engine about as well as anybody knew anything, I guess," George said.

> *All the time I worked on that steam engine, I never had any regrets. All in all, we had a good crew, and we gave that engine everything we knew how to give and succeeded and made a lot of people happy along the way. I could have stayed home, drew more money working elsewhere on the railroad, but there just is something about those old steam engines. There's nothing like them. And there was nothing like the One Spot.*

8

ALL ABOARD! FOR THE NO. 1'S EXCURSIONS

The Clinchfield Railroad, which had abandoned its last passenger train in 1955,
has found a new way of making money out of passenger traffic: put an 1882
steam locomotive out in front.
—the New York Times, *July 20, 1969*

With the shakedown trip a success, the Santa Train pulled and the Hatcher brothers signed on as permanent cab crew, what was the Clinchfield Railroad to do next with Tom Moore's celebrated new toy? First, there were three excursions slated from Erwin to Spruce Pine, North Carolina, for employees and retirees, the first on December 7, 1968, with 457 passengers spread over eight passenger cars, and the third and final on February 1, 1969. The employee trips, dubbed "Safety Specials," were the company's thank-you for hard work, but just as likely they were captive-audience tests for the planned public excursions. All employees were invited to take part, as were retirees and the widows of former employees. "Those who make the trip," Moore wrote to invitees, "will be my guests for a chicken dinner at Spruce Pine."

Much more would be expected of the newly refurbished No. 1 than a test run, a ride with Santa and three employee trips for chicken dinners—a lot more. Still, passenger service on the Clinchfield had been shuttered since 1955, so this new endeavor, pulled by an eighty-six-year-old steam engine, would require detailed planning.

"Reporters," H. Reid wrote, "doted on No. 1," and in turn, rail buffs and local residents were clamoring to hitch a ride. On December 30, 1968, Virginia Lingar of Kingsport, Tennessee, wrote:

November 23, 1968, was the day for the shakedown trip. The No. 1 pulled its tender and three passenger cars from Erwin to Kingsport and back. *Photo by David DeVault.*

Enveloped in a cloud of steam, P.O. Likens took a turn in the Clinchfield No. 1's cab on the engine's inaugural outing on November 23, 1968. *Photo by David DeVault.*

Gentlemen: We recently learned that the Clinchfield plans to make several excursions with its steam engine next summer. Please place our names on your list for these reservations for tickets when they become available to the general public. My father, Mr. W.W. Randolph, worked for the Clinchfield more than 35 years, so we have always been very close to the railroad. We would appreciate any information you could give us as to the proposed dates, starting points, destinations, prices and times and etc., of the planned excursions.

Superintendent J.L. Lonon replied a few days later, on January 3, 1969, writing:

Dear Mrs. Lingar, Your letter…has been passed on to me…and I must say we are very pleased to hear from our friends who are interested in the Railroad, particularly those who come from families that have been closely associated with the Company such as in your case. Our plans to operate an excursion for the general public at present are uncertain; however, should a train of this nature be operated, it would be given widespread publicity though the various news media and other special advertising arrangements, which would furnish all the information concerning dates, price, time, etc.

But the Clinchfield Railroad was, indeed, about to begin passenger service once again—in fact, the first excursion took place only five days after Lonon wrote to Mrs. Lingar. *Spartanburg Herald* editor Jim Oliphant documented the No. 1's January 8, 1969 push into the South Carolina city for its first public excursion under the headline, "The Past Drifts Back on Smoke and Cinders." The trip, a forty-minute ride from Chesnee, was "a colorful look at the past and a preview of things to come."

"A tiny locomotive huffed and puffed its way Wednesday into Spartanburg from the hills of Tennessee," Oliphant wrote. "Steam Engine No. 1, proud little workhorse veteran of the Clinchfield Railroad Co., has come out of retirement." From an interview with Moore, it was estimated the steam engine, over its life, had logged nearly 630,000 miles. The general manager intended to add to that figure substantially, and he said, for the first time publicly, that the railroad planned to inaugurate excursion runs from Spartanburg to Spruce Pine, North Carolina, a one-day round trip. For the January 8 outing, the No. 1 pulled only Moore's office car and an observation car, but he told Oliphant, the planned excursions would feature at least ten more cars, carrying up to five hundred passengers.

Over the next few months, several excursions did take place, all garnering praise from a public eager to see, hear and experience life on the rails behind a steam locomotive. Lonon's hesitation to detail plans for Mrs. Lingar was surely based on the scramble going on at the Clinchfield Railroad to fulfill the new general manager's plans and the uncertainties on how to make them happen. Only a few months later, Lonon was receiving letters from happy passengers. In a July 24 letter, A.M. Glasgow of Alexandria, Virginia, wrote:

> *I wanted to write and tell you how much I enjoyed the trip I took on your excursion of 20 July. This was one of the best I ever made. I hate to admit it, but the railroad personnel can run a better excursion than can the National Railway Historical Society. And I am a member. I think this is the greatest public relations idea a small railroad ever had. Look at the turn-out!...If you or your people are ever in Washington, please give me a call so I can entertain you as nicely as I was treated in Tennessee.*

General Manager Moore, Superintendent Lonon and transportation assistant John Lukianoff were all inundated with letters of adoration. The return to steam made a powerful impact. In a three-page, handwritten letter sent on August 14, Edward T. West of Hickory, North Carolina, wrote:

> *Your operating personnel were courteous, efficient and gave the appearance of being people who enjoyed their work and who were out to do more than just draw a day's pay. If the Postal Service, of which I am a member, could get their hands on whoever in your organization is responsible for the morale, devotion to duty, etc. that is apparent in your personnel, it would do well to pirate that person away from the Clinchfield.*

In a humble reply, Lonon assured Mr. West it was all a team effort, saying:

> *It is doubtful that any one person is responsible for the moral devotion of any of our employees, as the greater number of them are just high-caliber people of this nature and any credit certainly would have to be divided between all those who had anything to do with the operation of our train.*

It was clear Moore wanted his excursions to work perfectly, and it was up to his department heads to get the job done. Superintendent Lonon issued a memo on April 7, 1969, stressing just that. "The General Manager insists that the Passenger Trains scheduled for operations...be operated on schedule and without delay by other trains," he wrote. "Please see that the

Taking time to build up steam during the shakedown trip, the No. 1 made this stop near the town of Unicoi, a few miles from Erwin. *Photo by David DeVault.*

movement of these trains is given preference over that of other trains and dispatched without delay on our account."

As celebrated as the "new" Clinchfield No. 1 was, excursions needed more than an engine, so early on, Moore's supervisors set out to find passenger cars. Even before the work on the No. 1 was complete, superintendent Lonon had purchased two coaches from the Seaboard Coast Line Railroad Company, SCL 821 and 822. The Clinchfield took possession of them on November 14, 1968, at Miller Yard in Scott County, Virginia, and according to a Lonon memo, the cars were ordered to be moved to Erwin's mechanical department for service and inspection by "first suitable train." H. Reid details further that following the Seaboard purchases was a coach from the Nashville, Chattanooga & St. Louis and another from Louisville & Nashville. The ever-growing fleet of passenger cars was repainted in Pullman green with gold stripes. "I wanted the cars to look like another era," Moore once said. Soon a "club car," converted from an old mail car, was added. The *Piedmont* newspaper of Greenville, South Carolina, said the car "boasts railroad elegance in oak paneling, wall-to-wall carpeting, bar with a padded leather rim and a mural of Clinchfield's No. 1."

"The entire train," Robert G. Sargent continued in his *Piedmont* piece,

> *represents an outstanding example of railroading ingenuity. The club car*
> *was designed by the bartender and the locomotive, resplendent in gleaming*

black iron and trimmed in brass with highly polished drive wheels and pistons marks painstaking efforts of shop crews in restoring the engine after thirteen years of rusting away in a weed-grown graveyard…Public enthusiasm for the excursion trips has far exceeded expectations…and, consequently, old No. 1 has been pressed into much harder service than her builders anticipated. The ancient locomotive takes the punishment well.

The passenger cars' original windows, which could not be opened, were soon replaced by aluminum windows that could easily be raised. This made railfans happy, or as Dr. Herbert Spaugh wrote for the *Charlotte News*, "Every steam buff wants to be able to raise the window, look out and smell coal smoke from the locomotive." The Clinchfield aimed to please.

Writing in the August–September 1970 issue of the *Western Tar Heel Civitan*, Clinchfield press representative Bill Cannon recalled the scramble to put everything in place:

Then came cars—the Clinchfield had run its last passenger train in May 1955—and so the railroad turned to its neighbors for eleven coaches. They were refurbished and equipped with windows which will open so the passengers can hear the steamer work on the grades, and most of all, so they can hear the whistle sing happily out to the company's diesels that steam is still alive on a very modern Clinchfield. And the diesels listen too! They get out of the Number One's way when she is out on the line with the spick and span cars. The diesel upstarts are quite respectful in the presence of the oldest steam locomotive in this country operating in regular service on a railroad fortunate to have such spectacular scenery and fantastic construction details.

For all the hype, though, the Clinchfield No. 1 couldn't manage eleven modern passenger cars on its own. When it was built in 1882, the cars it pulled were made of wood, not steel and concrete, and some of the modern cars being brought in for the Clinchfield's mountain scenery excursions each could easily top the scales at one hundred tons or more. For the Santa Train and the safety specials, a diesel unit—an FP7A, No. 200, tucked in behind the No. 1 and its coal tender—had been needed to get the job done. While the power of the diesel helper was needed, of somewhat equal importance to Moore was the need to eliminate the very sight of it. Moore felt, correctly, that the gray-and-yellow diesel helper dampened the desired nostalgic scene the railroad wanted to paint with its revamped steamer. "He was," H. Reid

In Johnson City on the shakedown trip, Ed Hatcher chats with John "Kyle" Cacy, the rebuilding team's pilot. P.O. Likens provides a little oil. *Courtesy of the Nancy Moore Pearson Collection.*

wrote, "uneasy…of the streamlined backup engine showing over No. 1's low tender. It tampered with the old-time appearance he sought."

So, Reid continued, "to provide vital power, Clinchfield traded an F7B Motor unit to Louisville & Nashville for a steam-boilered FP7B, No. 723." The railroad renumbered this special diesel as No. 250 and, in another brilliant move, the masterful Clinchfield Railroad shop workers disguised it as a baggage car, painting it green, striped in gold, to match the passenger cars. Better yet, a crew wasn't needed to run the diesel backup—engineer Ed Hatcher did it all from his antique steam locomotive by using a homemade control box (designed by Clinchfield's general mechanical inspector Gene Bowman) mounted in the No. 1's cab. A second "B" unit, also disguised as a baggage car and listed as No. 869, was added to aid when even more power was needed. These two additional engines were referred to as "boosters" and gave the No. 1 extra power up steep mountain grades, but the diesel booster units supplied more than added oomph. The 250, for example, had a steam generator used to supply heat for the passenger cars. The 869 had a tank to carry extra water for the No. 1's tender, eliminating the need for stops along the way to take on more water for the antique steam engine.

As the passenger excursions got under way, memos traveled back and forth between Clinchfield Railroad department heads at a furious pace. A standard call-to-duty memo from road foreman R.E. Rice to chief dispatcher W.C. Reese would read, "Call Engineer T.E. Hatcher, Fireman G.L. Hatcher Jr., the Conductor first-out on the Conductor's Extra Board, and the Brakeman first-out on the Brakeman's Extra Board to man the Passenger Special." In typed correspondence usually spanning several pages, Superintendent Lonon would specify the train's arrival and departure times, both northward and southward, at all locations, as well as assembling instructions for the diesel units and the passengers cars. On use of the diesel locomotives with the No. 1, he wrote, "Must not be separated except in case of emergency or for servicing." On a planned stop, he wrote on July 4, 1969, "On arrival [in] Spruce Pine, train will be parked on the Work Track between crossover switches opposite the Spruce Pine Station, where passengers will detrain for lunch." On who was to oversee the train, he wrote on June 12, 1969, "Mr. [Ted] Stultz will accompany and be in complete charge of the train. Mr. Lukianoff will accompany the train, assist Mr. Stultz in any way possible, directing the Car Marshals, and handle other matters as may be directed."

And always ending:

> *This train must be dispatched effectively, operated on schedule and every precaution taken to protect the safety of passengers while en route, as well as boarding and detraining. Please give this matter your full and undivided attention to see that every detail is worked out so as to effect a safe and satisfactory operation.*

The Clinchfield workers not only had to run a train and board and detrain passengers, but also, as the excursions eventually became more elaborate, they had to purchase theater tickets, book hotel rooms and even charter buses. Almost all the excursions included a lunch of some sort, usually provided at a stop midway. Small eateries in North Carolina and Erwin were used in 1969, and it was evident that the staff had to work out details of feeding several hundred people. Receipts for hasty purchases of lemons, packets of tea and even coffee pots can be found in the railroad archives, proving that the 1969 excursions were a work in progress. In the spring of 1970, James Mahatzke, area director for Kentucky Fried Chicken in Greenville, South Carolina, approached the railroad with the idea of providing boxed meals for passengers. Management was intrigued. In a letter to Mahatzke, Lukianoff said, "Our Superintendent...has approved...use on our May 2nd trip, to see

One week after the shakedown trip, on November 30, 1968, the No. 1 pulled the Santa Train. Notice diesel engine No. 200 behind the No. 1 and tender. It was quickly replaced by a diesel designed to resemble a baggage car. This photo was taken near Starnes, Virginia. *Photo by David DeVault.*

just how this will work out. If this trial proves successful, I have no doubt that will be continued on our future trips." In return, the fried chicken chain, well known today but still an up-and-coming eatery in the early 1970s, proposed a boxed lunch of two pieces of chicken; four ounces of hot barbecue baked beans; four ounces of potato salad; two Colonel Sanders' rolls; one serving of iced tea with lemon, coffee, cold Pepsi or milk; and an individual cup of ice cream (three flavors). Each meal would cost one dollar and fifty cents plus tax. The plan was a success, and subsequent excursions often included Colonel Sanders's famous chicken, with similar deals struck with Kentucky Fried Chickens in other areas, including Erwin. Most passengers seemed pleased, although Samuel J. Boldrick of Atlanta, Georgia, sent a check for a fifteen-dollar round-trip ticket and advised, "I hate fried chicken. The Colonel Sanders here in Atlanta has a good fish dinner, and if I could have that instead of the chicken, I would be all smiles." Jim Kluttz, a columnist for the *Laurens County (South Carolina) Advertiser*, was apparently a fan of the colonel and spent much of his newspaper column talking about his lunch of fried chicken. Hungry by the time he reached Erwin, Kluttz wrote, "[Wife] Alma and I polished ours off and there wasn't enough left on the chicken bones to feed a gnat."

Souvenirs proved almost as important to passengers as their meals of finger-lickin'-good chicken, especially a Clinchfield Railroad patch and white

Pulling its first Santa Train, the Clinchfield No. 1 crosses the north fork of the Holston River. A diesel helper and one passenger car have been discarded for entrance back into Kingsport. *Photo by David DeVault.*

"engineer shop caps." Lukianoff noted to the distributer, Bosch Embroidery Inc. of Kansas City, Missouri, that "demand for these particular items is very heavy." Crew members who opted to wear their own white hats didn't keep them very long, as passengers offered to buy them and were even known to beg for one.

The early excursions were promoted heavily in local media, including newspaper advertisements that included a coupon to return to reserve seats. Tickets for an April 21, 1969 trip from Erwin to Kentucky and back were thirteen dollars each for adults and six dollars and fifty cents for children under twelve years old. The ad, under the header "FIRST CALL!," urged readers to snatch up tickets quickly.

When Superintendent Lonon wasn't handling details and correspondence for the excursions, the duties fell to the conscientious J.R. Lukianoff, the hardworking, newly named transportation assistant. Lukianoff, a Russian immigrant and New York transplant to Erwin, was Moore's hand-picked man to oversee the public work of the locomotive. H. Reid wrote that Lukianoff worked himself so thin he "didn't cast a shadow" but, nevertheless, became "an instant celebrity…due to a rare, outgoing personality." Files stored at the Archives of Appalachia contain dozens of letters Lukianoff wrote to potential customers, some seeking costs for excursions, others information or a photo or memento. There are so many letters to Lukianoff and copies of his cordial replies, in fact, that one wonders if the man ever left his typewriter.

Mostly importantly, Lukianoff's preserved letters provide invaluable insight into the Clinchfield's pleasure trips. On June 2, 1969, Lukianoff wrote to Bob Delium, recreation director for Tennessee Eastman Corporation, providing answers for possible excursions. An overnight trip from Kingsport, Tennessee, to Spartanburg, South Carolina, with a minimum of three hundred people would cost seventeen dollars per person and include a "boxed lunch put on the train at Spruce Pine, North Carolina, in each direction." A one-day excursion from Kingsport to Kentucky, with a guarantee of three hundred people that would include lunch, would be offered at a cost of seven dollars per head.

In 1970, H. Reid said Lukianoff's "effervescent conversation" was responsible for forty outings to drum up business from children's camps, civic clubs and industrial groups.

Maintaining costs was important. In a May 8, 1969 memo from superintendent Lonon to general manager Moore, the main engine and train crew costs were outlined for three routes. For the 136-mile Erwin-to-Elkhorn, Kentucky route, costs were: for conductor, $33.18; for brakeman, $30.08; for engineer, $33.67; and for fireman, $29.44. For the 141-mile Erwin-to-Spartanburg, South Carolina route, payroll was: for conductor, $34.27; for brakeman, $31.07; for engineer, $34.77; and for fireman, $30.39. For the 196-mile Spartanburg-to-Spruce Pine, North Carolina and return outings, crew costs were: for conductor, $46.23; for brakeman, $41.98; for engineer, $46.90; and for fireman, $40.80. With payroll taxes, the most expensive route for the four main positions totaled just $220.39.

The excursion train wasn't just running on public adoration, as it was producing a tidy profit, too. The *New York Times* reported that from May 1 until mid-July 1969, more than ten thousand passengers had ridden behind the No. 1. "We didn't dream it would develop as well as it has," General Manager Moore told the *Times*. By the end of the year, more than sixteen thousand passengers had bought tickets.

The July 4 and 5 trip in 1969 was sold out weeks before steaming out of Spartanburg, and a report from Lukianoff to Moore and Lonon for the July 4 and 5, 1970 trip shows that excursion did equally well, producing $6,577.25 in ticket sales from a total of 784 passengers. The working personnel for the two days totaled thirty-eight, and that included twenty Unicoi County High School band parents manning the concession stand.

The excursions brought joy to thousands riding through the Appalachians from Tennessee to Kentucky, across the valleys of Virginia, to the mountains of the Carolinas and beyond. *Courtesy of the Kenneth Fortune Collection.*

The Clinchfield No. 1 emerges from Vance Tunnel, one of fifty-five tunnels on the Clinchfield Route, near Altapass, North Carolina, on September 11, 1971. *Photo by Roger Cook.*

Beginning in 1970, the Clinchfield got out of the ticket-selling business and put excursions into the hands of chartering organizations such as civic clubs and railfan excursions. The railroad simply offered the service of operating the train. This proved to be hugely successful for all parties. Chartering organizations raised money by selling excursion tickets, thus raising money for myriad projects, including children's hospitals, speech and hearing clinics, senior citizens' centers, boys' and girls' homes, orphanages and summer camps, as well as membership organizations such as Civitan clubs or railfan societies.

Throughout the years, passenger numbers continued to increase, as interest in the train—and its potential for fundraising opportunities—grew. An excursion on October 27 and 28, 1973, co-sponsored by the Breakfast Optimist Club of Spartanburg and the American Business Club, produced ticket sales in excess of $10,500. A memo from the Clinchfield's auditor showed that every October excursion had a minimum of 516 passengers, with the best being 647 on October 13.

Comparing the new numbers with those of the final years of regular passenger service on the Clinchfield in the early 1950s, one must wonder if Moore and company had been in charge then, would passenger service have ever been halted? Total passenger service revenue for 1951, 1952 and 1953 was $43,863.09. Total ticket sales for 1969, the first full year of excursions, was astonishing. A November 10, 1969 report compiled by Lukianoff showed a total of forty excursions had taken place with ticket sales totaling $111,194.75. H. Reid estimated the profit from those ticket sales to be more than $31,000.00.

By the mid-1970s, the railroad was routinely leasing full excursion trains to groups. In 1974, the charter rate for the No. 1 to pull from Marion, North Carolina, to Erwin was $4,500 for the steamer, its two diesel aids and eleven passenger cars with enough seating for 574 passengers. Groups could add the opulent White Oak observation car (No. 114) for another $250 and an additional twenty-five seats. A steam-only trip—the No. 1 only and two coaches with no aid from diesel boosters—could fetch as much as $3,000. By 1976, total annual sales from charter leases had exceeded $200,000.

Among the groups chartering trips behind No. 1 were various chapters of the National Railway Historical Society from Georgia, Virginia, the Carolinas and beyond; Eastman, the Sertoma Club of Spartanburg; the Breakfast Optimist Club of Spartanburg; the Rock Hill Junior Women's Club; the Drayton Ruritan Club; Civitan Clubs from Virginia, the Carolinas and Tennessee; the Burke County Rescue Squad; the Greenwood Jaycees;

the Bluegrass Model Railroad Club of Lexington, Kentucky; and dozens of others.

So what was it like for passengers aboard Moore's scenic mountain railway? According to Clinchfield Railroad documents, the passenger train would feature "reclining seat coaches, a parlor observation car and a lounge car." The observation car, called the "White Oak" after Moore's hometown, was a bit of luxury on the rails. Before coming to the Clinchfield, the car was the "City of Lafayette" and operated through Indiana (and close to the One Spot's birthplace) as part of the famed Wabash Cannon Ball. The pleasure of rail travel was, the Clinchfield bragged, "in addition to the wonderful scenery as one traverses the Blue Ridge Mountains and the Nolichucky River Gorge amid the artistic colors of Mother Nature's paint brush." A 1972 Clinchfield news release beckoned travelers to "experience the romance of yesteryear and enjoy the spectacular scenic beauty of the Blue Ridge Mountains on the 'railroad in the sky.'"

"CLINCHFIELD ONE, a standard gauge 'steamer' makes one-day trips and weekend excursion trips," the release went on to say. "A great delight for children from eight to eighty. Try it...you'll love it." A promotional poster produced that same year showing the No. 1 and train crossing the Catawba River Viaduct beckoned vacationers to "Ride the Fabled Clinchfield One."

Once the Clinchfielders had the excursion trains operating smoothly, very little changed, other than price increases when necessary. After the first year, a public address system was added to provide a commentator the ability to offer historical insight and various points of interest along the route. "Other than that," Lukianoff once wrote, "we are still operating in the same cordial manner."

Some of the most popular sojourns were the excursions between Erwin, Tennessee, and Spartanburg, South Carolina. These trips included more than a ride on the rails, with passengers also treated to overnight hotel stays, dinners and special events. The Friday, September 29, 1972 excursion, for example, was billed as a "fine package...for a weekend of fun and entertainment." Operating at this time as "the Clinchfield Special," the excursion train left Erwin at 12:30 p.m. and arrived in Spartanburg about five hours later. Upon arriving in Spartanburg, the passengers "detrained" and were bused to motels that had signed up to take advantage of the economic boon created by the little train from the mountains of Northeast Tennessee.

Passengers got first-class treatment with their luggage being delivered for them directly to their hotels. After a "freshening-up period" of an hour or

It wasn't just the passengers who enjoyed the train. Note the family on the right waving as the Clinchfield No. 1 steams by. *Photo by David DeVault.*

so, passengers again boarded buses for transportation to Greenville, South Carolina, for a performance by famed American trumpeter and bandleader Charlie Spivak and a "luxurious" dinner at Ye Old Fireplace, a restaurant-nightclub owned by Spivak and Charlie Grubbs. Following the performance by Spivak, billed by the Clinchfield as "the one and only," and his orchestra, passengers returned to their motels. They were treated to breakfast the next morning while their luggage was once again loaded aboard the train for their return trip to Erwin. A snack luncheon was served aboard the train at about midday at Spruce Pine, North Carolina.

Tennessee and Virginia "Theatre Special" packages proved immensely popular with passengers, who received overnight accommodations when attending shows at Tennessee's Olde West Dinner Theatre or Virginia's historic and acclaimed Barter Theatre in Abingdon (which counts among its former actors Ernest Borgnine, Gregory Peck, Hume Cronyn and Patricia Neal) with delicious meals provided at the opulent Martha Washington Inn just across the street. "Fall Color" specials ran in autumn when the canopies of forests along the railroad tracks turned orange, yellow and red hues against a backdrop of purple-hazed mountains.

A nice overview of the Clinchfield No. 1 and its excursion train, which gained popularity with every passing year. *Photo by David DeVault.*

A three-day golf excursion in 1972 had a high expense account but, likely, an even better return. The Clinchfield spent more than $7,600 for green fees and carts for one hundred golfers, boxed lunches, motel accommodations, buses to the course, crew, car marshals and more.

A newspaper advertisement under the header "Clinchfield Route" invited potential customers to "ride the most scenic route east of the Rockies through the scenic countryside and mountains behind the oldest steam locomotive still in active service in this country."

Passenger service was so popular that the railroad maintained a computerized mailing list that had grown to as many as 7,781 entries by the mid-1970s. An article in the *New York Times* on May 17, 1970 (the second time in less than a year the Clinchfield excursions were featured in the venerable publication), brought a barrage of inquiries from all over the world. Immediately, Lukianoff was sent scurrying to his typewriter to pound out replies to letters received from Weston, Massachusetts; Atlanta, Georgia; Northfield, Connecticut; Sullivan, Illinois; Hamtramck, Michigan; Iwakuni, Japan; Randfontein, Transvaal, South Africa; and many more.

Moore was ecstatic with the success of the excursions. In a short letter he wrote, the general manager's joy at the endeavor's success is clear:

> *Response to running Clinchfield No. 1 has been more than gratifying. The press, particularly, has been kind to me…*
> *We have had good fortune and good help.*
> *Percy Likens knows his machinery.*
> *Ed and George Hatcher know how to run it.*
> *John Lukianoff knows people.*
> *We want to thank all of the wonderful patrons who have visited us on numerous occasions and have made Clinchfield No. 1 a huge success.*

9
THE CLINCHFIELD SPECIAL

During the eleven years the Clinchfield No. 1 passenger excursions were offered, there were three distinct eras, all noted by the No. 1's coal tender. In 1968 and part of 1969, the tender was marked simply, but boldly, "CLINCHFIELD." From May 1969 until 1973, the train was marked as the "Clinchfield Special," with a new, not-so-bold script font. For the remainder of its tenure, from 1973 until 1979, the coal tender took on a more garish but corporate-friendly look with "The Family Lines" in yellow in the center and SCL, L&N, Clinchfield and Georgia, the corporation's various entities, displayed underneath in black lettering over a yellow bar.

The change from Clinchfield to the "Clinchfield Special" was the end result of a contest for employees and their families. Transportation assistant J.R. Lukianoff made the announcement on May 21, 1969. In a letter addressed to "all concerned," he wrote:

> The "NAME THE TRAIN" contest comes to a happy ending! Since the contest was instituted on February 1 of this year, a search for a suitable name for the "old No. 1 Spot" has been under way. After much deliberation by the judges, who were selected by the General Manager, Mr. T.D. Moore Jr., the winning entry selected, based on earliest date received, was "THE CLINCHFIELD SPECIAL." The winning entry was submitted by Mrs. E.T. Ellis, wife of one of the Clinchfield road conductors. The name will be put on the steam engine and hereafter will be referred to in any and all excursion trips as "THE CLINCHFIELD SPECIAL"...Several persons submitted the name,

An all-steam trip to Spartanburg, South Carolina, took place on January 8, 1969, and set in motion excursions for the next decade. *Courtesy of Martha Erwin/Clinchfield Railroad Museum.*

The No. 1 in Spruce Pine, North Carolina, in 1969. Note that the coal tender now says "Clinchfield Special," the result of a contest to rename the excursions. *Photo by Dave Beach.*

"THE CLINCHFIELD SPECIAL," but Mrs. Ellis' entry was the first received in this office.

As the winner, she received fifty dollars in cash.

Not all employees were happy with the name change, in particular Karl Thomas, who had been a member of the rebuilding team for the No. 1 and the coal tender before transferring to the Clinchfield's operations in Spartanburg, South Carolina. Thomas often found his weekends disrupted by the passenger excursions arriving in Spartanburg. "It actually got to be kind of a headache for me," he said. "I had to be on the job when the train came in. I had to be there until they got ready to go out the next morning, and I had to be there the following morning when it went out. It seems like every time my family had plans for the weekend, I had to work for the excursion. It upset our plans a lot. So when they had the contest to name it, I turned in the 'Excedrin Headache No. 1.'" Not surprisingly, Thomas's suggestion failed to win over the judges, as did an off-the-cuff review of the newly repainted coal tender.

"When they first rebuilt the engine," Thomas recalled,

> they painted the name *CLINCHFIELD* on the coal tender in really nice, old-style letters like the original, which was beautiful, but then they changed it when they renamed it the Clinchfield Special. After they put the Clinchfield Special on it, there was several of us down there one night talking about it, and we didn't really like it. And Mr. Moore was down there, but I didn't know it. He was probably just ten feet away, and I made some kind of statement about the Clinchfield Special being on the tender. Mr. Moore came up to me and said, "Well, what do you think of the paint job?" And I said, "Looks to me like some kid did it with a can of spray paint." He gave me a look and a growl and walked off. Then Mr. Likens came along, and I asked him, "Whose idea was this?" And he said, "Mr. Moore's. Why?" I told him, "I think I just made a bunch of points—the wrong ones." I absolutely did not like it. It just didn't look right. It didn't match the rest of the engine.

Thomas also didn't know Likens himself had applied the new name to the tender, using manually crafted stencils, according to H. Reid.

Passenger Roger Cook, in correspondence for this book, was also not happy with the change. "I…was disappointed to see 'Clinchfield Special' on the tender. I much preferred the original livery I'd seen in photos. However,

Stops for passengers to snap photos were scheduled during excursions, as shown here from a September 1978 excursion. *Photo by Mike Noonkestor.*

'Clinchfield Special' was much better than the 'Family Lines' billboard that later appeared."

As for the contest, H. Reid also noted that other entries included "Nolichucky Queen" and "Pride of the Clinchfield," as well as names referencing the No. 1's born-again status, including "Lazarus" and "the Survivor."

10

THE INVALUABLE P.O. LIKENS

Tom Moore may have been the savior of the Clinchfield No. 1, but it was chief mechanical officer Percy O. "P.O." Likens who brought the engine back to life. He even had the uncanny ability to make the old girl "talk."

Likens took great pride in working for the Clinchfield and wanted those around him to feel the same. As a Clinchfield apprentice, he had worked on the No. 1 when it came from Black Mountain to Erwin for routine service. His chance to oversee its regeneration in 1968 must have reinforced his love of steam. *Railroading* magazine noted in a 1969 article that Likens, even in the diesel era, kept a copy of Ralph P. Johnson's technical treatise *The Steam Locomotive* on his desk.

Everette Allen, who worked aboard the No. 1's excursions in the maintenance department, recalled how "invaluable" Likens was to the Clinchfield. "P.O. knew everything about the No. 1," Allen said, "and if there was anything we didn't know, he'd guide us through it. He was a gentleman's gentleman. He loved the Clinchfield No. 1. Loved it. Loved everything about it. You could tell it was just a part of him, the way he was made up."

P.O.'s son, Bob Likens, a Clinchfield trainmaster, had the opportunity to work beside his father and shared some tales from the rails in 2010 with East Tennessee State University student Sally Jackson for an oral history project with the George L. Carter Railroad Museum.

"One of the greatest stories we have was of the trip we took in July 1978," Bob told Jackson. "It was a 2,300-mile trip down in Florida and back…While we were coming back through Atlanta, Georgia, the ash pan underneath the

P.O. Likens assists Chi Cook of Oradell, New Jersey, on June 10, 1978. Likens had retired but often traveled with the Clinchfield No. 1's excursions. *Photo by Roger Cook.*

firebox, which catches the cinders and hot ashes from the firebox, one end of it comes down. And every time we'd go over a road crossing, it would hit the road crossing and hit up against the bottom of the engine. It sounded like the whole bottom engine was coming out."

Although retired, P.O. had stayed on as a "mechanical consultant" and often rode No. 1's excursions. "We had to take the engine off the train and pull it into the Atlanta shop to find somebody that would go under the engine and tighten up the ash pan," Bob continued. "Well we pulled into the shop, and most of the youngsters there were machinists and boilermakers. Probably some of them had never seen a steam engine before, and we didn't have any pits or anything to put the engine over. Somebody had to go underneath that hot engine. Now remember this is a hot engine, just came in off a run, smoke still coming out the stack, steam out both sides. My father was sixty-eight years old. He looked at me and said, 'Son go back and get my coveralls for me.' So I went back in the cars and got Dad's work clothes."

P.O. looked up at engineer Ed Hatcher and said, "Eddie, I'm going under the engine. Tighten that up. Don't let her move."

"Chief," Ed replied, "I got her tied down and won't move an inch till I hear from you."

With that, P.O. laid down on his back and slid under the engine. "All we could see was his feet sticking out over the rail," Bob recalled.

What seemed like to me was a long time was probably no more than five or six minutes. He came back out, tightened it up. We had to get the cinders off of him. He had some burns…in his clothes where the hot ashes had fallen on him. He walked up and patted the old No. 1 on the side and said, "You're all right now, gal." And about that time the steam engine popped off steam. Went, "Pewsh, Pewsh" just exactly like she said, "Thank you." Well, everybody around there laughed about it. We call that the time that No. 1 said, "Thank you." That was one of the greatest stories we have.

11

PUBLIC RELATIONS

Marketing for Rosebud's excursions was a top priority for the Clinchfield Railroad, especially in 1969, when the first public excursions were held. Newspapers and magazines as far away as the *Miami Herald* in Florida routinely sent in advertising requests, hoping to cash in on the Clinchfield Railroad's well-oiled marketing machine. Beyond advertising dollars, though, the Clinchfield Railroad depended on word of mouth to fill passenger cars. Media advertising departments may have been eager to add the Clinchfield to their client lists, but the news departments were just as captivated by the little steam engine. If the Clinchfield No. 1 was coming to town, it made the front pages of newspapers everywhere, and the Clinchfield Railroad banked on nostalgia to sell seats.

W.C. "Mutt" Burton, a celebrated staff writer and columnist with North Carolina's *Greensboro Daily News*, took a different twist on the traditional news story and wrote in the Sunday, October 19, 1969 edition something of a soliloquy titled "Autumn Journey":

> *Dawn rests mistily on the mountains. A steam locomotive, ancient but impatient, snorts vapors into the cool air. It coughs with quiet dignity, strains, moves. The whistle shouts. A journey into Appalachian autumn.*
>
> *The sky is mid-October blue, the clouds small and lustrous as clusters of pearls. Up the Blue Ridge slope, valleys falling away into blue shadows, the world's rim high and distant. Then the winking surprise of tunnels. The train dives in and out of darkness. The brilliant scene blinks on and off.*

WRTV from Indianapolis, Indiana, films the Clinchfield No. 1 in Erwin on June 8, 1974, before the train is set to depart to Altapass, North Carolina. *Photo by Roger Cook.*

They call it the Fall Color Train—a long ride into nostalgia in the Land of the Sky. The train rolls through valley and height from Marion to Erwin, Tennessee.

In the mountains, the Clinchfield Railroad is a storied one. And an old steam engine pulls the train that takes us on an excursion into beauty.

Girls peddle candy and drinks. The passengers gaze out, settle back, enjoying the dual delights of nature and nutty bars. Cold Cokes in hand, they suck at scenery and straws. Bright fall unfolds like the pages of a fantastic picture book.

Dark evergreens set the foliage gems. Ruby reds of dogwood and blackgum. Deep garnet of sumac. Golden topaz of hickory, ash, birch, locust, tulip poplar. Sparkling filigree of Virginia creeper. Mixed sunbursts of maples.

Rivers rush nearby, silver in sunlight, amethyst in shallows, onyx in shady deeps.

Rich colors foam on the slopes, surge against the peaks. A white farmhouse catches the sunset, trees like torches in the farmyard. Shadows gather again in the valley, planning the night.

The names of places—some are strange—but they are all eloquent and they speak of half-forgotten days that float like mist across the hills.

Boonford. "Frankie and Johnny were sweethearts" and Frankie slew her cheating spouse. Now the mountain entombs them both, a great bejeweled crypt.

Kona feldspar, kaolin and mica.

Relief. Once it had the only doctor for miles, thus gaining its therapeutic name.

Lost Cove. The lonely legend of lost people. The wild beauty of Nolichucky River Gorge.

Picnic in a Tennessee mountain churchyard. The vestibule view is a turnabout; it is the outside world that glows with cathedral colors.

"Oh, Suzannah, don't you cry for me,
I'm rolling on the Clinchfield line back home from Tennessee."

Advertisements frequently appeared in northeast Tennessee newspapers, like the *Johnson City Press-Chronicle* and the *Erwin Record*, to attract locals to embrace their railroad heritage and spend a day riding the rails. The railroad went beyond the Tri-Cities of Tennessee, though, advertising in newspapers in the Carolinas, Georgia and beyond and making sure to take advantage of special editions such as the *Charlotte (North Carolina) Observer*'s "Vacation in the Mountains."

Success for the multi-point "Theatre Specials" depended on a good marketing plan and coordination. Dr. Robert Porterfield, founder and director at Abingdon, Virginia's historic Barter Theatre, was eager for the guests and the added publicity the Clinchfield provided the official "state theater of Virginia." In an April 17, 1970 letter to Porterfield, transportation assistant John Lukianoff wrote, "It is our intent to have two theatre trips this year, the first being on Saturday, June 13th, and the second on Saturday, October 3rd. Based on the success of the venture last year, and with the interest of quite a number of persons expressed so far this year, we have definitely placed these trips on our agenda." A large ad was placed in the

May 25, 1970 issue of the *Atlanta Journal* promoting the "Theatre Special." "Relax and Enjoy," the ad exclaimed. It continued:

> *One of the most delightful weekends of your life can begin the morning of June 13. Ride behind Clinchfield Number 1…along Toe River… under Lost Cove and other spectacular Blue Ridge Mountain scenery. See the delightful play* Plaza Suite *(now on Broadway), at historic Barter Theatre and dine at picturesque Martha Washington Inn in Abingdon, Virginia. Only $140 per couple. Leave Spartanburg, S.C., 9:00 a.m., Saturday, June 12, return to Spartanburg 4:30 p.m. Sunday, June 14.*

It's interesting to note the tourism dollars generated by the Clinchfield excursions. The "Theatre Specials" alone brought visitors to four states over two days: the Carolinas and into Tennessee with stays at hotels in the Tri-Cities and, finally, into Virginia for the destination. Claude Callaway, representing Firestone Textiles Company of Spartanburg, wrote to the Clinchfield in the spring of 1970 expressing his hope that the theater excursions would continue. "The trips last year surely were a great tourist undertaking," Callaway wrote. "We need more of such attractions."

The Spartanburg Chamber of Commerce was eager to assist the Clinchfield. Chamber officials offered up everything from art exhibitions and planetarium tours to a peach-picking jaunt and a Wofford football game. Local hotels like the Holiday Inn, Motor Inn, Ramada Inn and Rodeway Inn expressed interest in accommodating train passengers during overnight excursions.

In 1971, general manager Tom Moore invited media outlets from all over the Carolinas to experience the Clinchfield's "Theatre Specials" and booked hotel stays for the reporters, photographers and cameramen, as well as their spouses. Guests represented television stations WIS and WOLO in Columbia, WFBC and WLOS in Greenville, WBTV and WSOC in Charlotte, radio stations WIS in Columbia and WMRB in Greenville and a host of newspapers such as the *State* and the *Record* (both of Columbia), the *Piedmont* and the *News* (both of Greenville), the *Daily Star* of Shelby, the *Gazette* of Gastonia, the *Record* of Hickory, the *Ledger* of Gaffney, the *Newberry Observer*, the *Index Journal* of Greenwood, the *Evening Herald* of Rock Hill, the *News-Herald* of Winnsboro, the *Charlotte Observer*, the *Times-Democrat* of Orangeburg and the *Herald* of Spartanburg. Gary Womack and his wife, Ann, with the South Carolina Department of Parks, Recreation and Tourism, were also guests. While in the region, the guests were treated to a show and meal at the Olde West Dinner Theatre. Robert G. Sergent, writing

Passengers were treated to breathtaking vistas high above the Appalachian hills and valleys.
Photo by David DeVault.

for the *Piedmont*, wrote, "SPARTANBURG—Clinchfield No. 1 was standing at a siding here, a few wisps of steam wafting skyward, when the first of 50 newsmen and their wives arrived Saturday for a two-day railroading jaunt… It was to be a fascinating trip…If you haven't climbed aboard Clinchfield's No. 1, even for a one-day excursion, you've missed one of the most delightful vacation attractions the Carolinas have to offer." The subsequent media coverage filled passenger seats for months and added to the allure of the Clinchfield Railroad.

Marketing got a massive push outside the South, too—a three-page travel piece in the *Chicago Tribune*'s April 30, 1972 edition. The article detailed where readers could enjoy steam train excursions in Kentucky, Virginia, West Virginia, North Carolina, South Carolina, Tennessee, Georgia and Florida. For the Clinchfield, the *Tribune* wrote:

> *The normally "freight-only" line has been chugging over its…miles of track with an ancient steam engine—the oldest one still operating in the country—that pulls vintage coaches thru some of the best scenery in the East. Trips are scheduled from time to time during the summer and fall over the entire line, which snakes thru five states—Kentucky, Tennessee, Virginia and North and South Carolina. The rail line crosses a 2,653-foot-high pass over the Eastern Continental Divide, follows Nolichucky Gorge, and meanders thru the Pisgah and Cherokee National Forests. There are 55 tunnels, totaling nearly 10 miles in length, on the system.*

Perhaps the most extensive news coverage at a single time came in November 1973, when the *New York Times* news service wrote a story about the Clinchfield No. 1 and the annual Santa Train. Not only was the piece published in the *Times*, but newspapers across the world also carried it, including the *Hawaii Tribune Herald*, the *Baltimore Sun*, the *Atlanta Journal*, the *Arkansas Gazette*, the *Cincinnati Enquirer*, the *Miami News* and dozens more.

"We're getting a lot of favorable publicity out of the No. 1," General Manager Moore told *Sandlapper* magazine. His daughter, Nancy Moore Pearson, said her father wanted the Clinchfield to stand out among all the companies in the Family Lines corporation. "He felt that the Clinchfield didn't always get its due recognition in terms of the profit that it generated," she said,

> *because it was extremely profitable for the Family Lines, for Seaboard Coast Lines…He wanted the Clinchfield to shine. When he flew to New York as a board member of the greater company, he wanted the people who worked*

for him to stand out. One way of making sure they got their due recognition was to have a little good PR…He thought of the No. 1 as goodwill and a way to be a good neighbor, as it were, and a way for people to look at the railroad as a good thing as opposed to you have to sit in your car and wait for the train to pass…The whole business of riding on a train never seemed very romantic to me until the steam engine came along, and then that was a whole new ball of wax. People loved, just loved, being on the train. When I was at home from college and before I left, he insisted that I go on the excursions…Daddy would walk up and down through all the cars, meeting people and shaking hands, and I was right there with him. It was fascinating to see him and how responsive people were and how much they loved being there. Obviously, the PR of the No. 1 was working. People were so happy.

12

"DISASTER" ON THE CLINCHFIELD

The press and word of mouth were the best of friends to the Clinchfield No. 1 for most of its time on the rails and for its jolly jaunts through the mountains. But on one occasion, the headlines seemed more like something out of Agatha Christie's *Murder on the Orient Express*. Well, not quite, but this June 1975 headline from the *McDowell News*—"Food Suspect in Train Poisoning Incident"—left Clinchfield public relations officers scrambling. Unlike most of the happy days aboard the No. 1's excursions, June 14, 1975, was anything but pleasurable. The *McDowell News*, the local newspaper in Marion and most often a cheerleader for the old Clinchfield, dedicated most of its front page on June 16 to stories and photos under the blaring headline from above, and not even the most heavily scripted Clinchfield public relations man could control the spin when nearly 20 percent of the passengers on the "Rhododendron Special" roundtrip excursion from Spartanburg, South Carolina, to Erwin, Tennessee, became violently ill—a case, it seemed, of food poisoning.

According to various newspaper reports, the first call for emergency assistance came at about 5:25 p.m. on Saturday, June 14, near Marion, North Carolina, about four hours after passengers "had reportedly eaten a box lunch at the Clinchfield Railway Terminal in Erwin." Dean Wall, communications director for the McDowell County Rescue Squad, said authorities were asked to meet the train, which was making its return trip to Spartanburg, South Carolina, from Erwin. The *McDowell News* also sourced Imogene Poole, director of nursing at Marion General, saying the first patients, "being transported by local ambulance, rescue squad, law

It was around this location, nearing Marion, North Carolina, where some passengers became very ill. Railroad personnel had radioed ahead, and medical crews were awaiting the train. *Courtesy of the Kenneth Fortune Collection.*

enforcement, fire departments, and individuals," arrived about 6:00 p.m. "They first told us there would be about twenty-five persons, but before it was over, we had administered ninety-five IVs," Poole said, adding that patients were as young as three and as old as seventy. A list of patients, found at East Tennessee State University's Archives of Appalachia, however, shows the oldest patient treated at Marion was seventy-four. The *Asheville Citizen* reported in its June 17 issue that out of ninety-five people treated, thirty-one were admitted to hospitals. "About twenty-five patients were held overnight and released Sunday morning," the *Citizen* wrote, "including about seven people who were transferred from an overflowing Marion General Hospital to Grace Hospital in Morganton." The numbers vary, depending on the source. The *McDowell News*, for example, has the number of admitted higher. "In less than two hours," the newspaper wrote, "forty-two of the ninety-five persons treated had been admitted for further observation. Twenty-five of those forty-two were to remain overnight and six were transferred to Grace Hospital in Morganton. The train continued on to Spartanburg around 7:00 p.m., but upon arrival back in South Carolina, fifteen persons, one admitted, were taken to Spartanburg Memorial Hospital." Again, numbers vary, with the *Citizen* putting the Spartanburg number at twenty, not fifteen.

In total, four hospitals—Marion General Hospital and Grace Hospital in North Carolina and Barnwell County Hospital and Spartanburg General Hospital in South Carolina—treated patients. Reports also indicated as many as ten doctors and thirty-five off-duty hospital personnel responded. But Clinchfield spokesman Bob Lusby did very little talking and attempted to put the blame on caterers and not the Clinchfield by saying, "It was just a normal excursion. The food was catered by an outside service." Perhaps later placed in the better-to-have-not-made-a-comment file, Lusby "declined to comment" to the *News Herald* of Morganton, North Carolina, before adding—and being quoted, of course, "This type of thing is not conducive to good public relations with the public."

Try as he might, Lusby could not contain the story. Sick passengers trapped aboard a slow-moving excursion train winding through the mountainous curves of the Carolinas was too juicy for any good reporter. In addition to the *News Herald*, the *McDowell News*, the *Asheville Citizen* and the *Asheville Times* all headlining the story, the Associated Press also put a story on the wire, which meant newspapers across the country were able to pick up the unfortunate tale. Not hampered by modern privacy laws, hospital and emergency personnel were more than forthcoming to reporters, who detailed the story without Lusby's aid. The total number of sick varied, depending on the source. The *McDowell News* gave the total of sick at 110 out of 595 passengers. Dr. George G. Ellis, one of the McDowell County physicians called to the Marion depot to meet the train, estimated that at least "one-fifth"—or 20 percent—of the train's passengers became sick, the *Asheville Citizen* reported, adding that Wall was initially told only 23 people aboard were sick. "But," the newspaper reported, "by the time the train reached Marion, the number had grown to ninety-five. Dr. Ellis said more than twenty other passengers had become ill and in need of treatment by the time it reached Spartanburg." An unnamed physician aboard the train was also said to have cared for the ill until Marion could be reached.

Media reports indicated that the prime suspect was the catered meal of ham, baked beans and potato salad passengers received once reaching Erwin. Most of the ill experienced vomiting and severe diarrhea. Dr. Ellis told the *McDowell News* that any of the food items "could have been contaminated." The food awaiting passengers upon their arrival in Erwin would have acted, the doctor said, "almost like incubators" for germs. One passenger, Dr. Ellis said, claimed the train was ninety minutes late arriving in Erwin, but the railroad denied there was a late arrival, and adamantly, Lusby said, "I was standing there when it came in." The Hatcher brothers ran a time-efficient train, so it seems doubtful the train was extremely late arriving in Erwin. To prove his point in denying the late arrival, Lusby said the train left Spartanburg at 8:30 a.m., arrived in Erwin at 1:00 p.m. and departed for the return trip one hour later, at 2:00 p.m. "It takes about four and one-half hours to cover the 144-mile trip each way. I'll agree that it takes a little more time here in the mountains, but not that much more."

The Clinchfield's excursion team quickly set about making sure passengers, whether hospitalized or not, received good care. The railroad paid for motel rooms, either at the Holiday Inn, the Lemon Tree Inn or Gibb's Motel, for those who opted not to continue by train (the train, under diesel power only, left Marion a few hours later to continue on to Spartanburg) or for family members with loved ones admitted to the hospital.

A number of patient records from that eventful day are stored at the Archives of Appalachia. Several patient files are slugged atop, by hospital personnel, with the words "Clinchfield Railroad Disaster." Perhaps that was a bit grandiose, but for the usually profitable and stress-free excursions, it was a major disappointment. Reimbursement to passengers for their medical expenses totaled in the thousands. In a letter to Lusby on June 17, Marion

Excursions from Spartanburg to Erwin often included lunch in Erwin. Tables were set up in the parking lot between the Erwin Railroad Station and the Clinchfield Railroad headquarters. *Courtesy of the Kenneth Fortune Collection.*

General Hospital controller Lucille F. Conley wrote, "Enclosed is [*sic*] copies of individual accounts for each patient treated during the Food Poisoning on June 14, 1975…We sincerely hope our services were satisfactory, and that all your passengers have fully recuperated." Those services alone totaled $3,726.50. In addition to medical bills, the railroad contracted with Continental Trailways for buses, at several hundred dollars, to transport passengers left behind in Marion to Spartanburg.

Throughout the ordeal, railroad personnel were keeping up with the ever-changing situation by making notes on scraps of paper and motel stationery—a good thing, too, since general manager T.D. Moore sent a carefully written memo on June 24 to make sure the company had been meticulous in record keeping. "In view of the fact that the Clinchfield may have to take some legal action for reimbursement of extra expenses incurred because of the incident occurring on June 14 in connection with the excursion train," Moore wrote, "it is most important that you keep an accurate record of these expenses incurred by your respective department, having them ready when called for." Nothing in archived files, however, indicates if the railroad faced any lawsuits or if it, in fact, filed suit against a caterer.

A few passengers wrote letters after the excursion, seeking items left behind on the train. The Hudsons, for example, of Hendersonville,

North Carolina, had left behind several items of clothing, a set of binoculars and a cooler. They were, nevertheless, appreciative of those who took care of the sick, calling the medical aid received in Marion "above reproach."

Perhaps, then, in the end, Imogene Poole summed it up best: "All the people left complimentary and appreciative. It could have been a total disaster."

As if transporting sick passengers was not bad enough, the Clinchfield No. 1 also fell ill during the trip, although only one of the several newspaper accounts of the food-poisoning "disaster" mentions the locomotive's breakdown, and even then, the *McDowell News* devoted only two paragraphs to the engine's woes: "Upon direct questioning, Lusby did confirm, however, that the train was delayed about 30 to 40 minutes just north of the Catawba River 'reservoir' after the request for emergency aid." Besieged with sick passengers, probing reporters and anxious railroad officials, Lusby gave an overwhelmingly inadequate answer when he told the newspaper, "We did have trouble with our little steam engine." Details of the No. 1's mechanical troubles came to light the following week when an excursion on June 21, 1975, for the East Tennessee Rail Fan Association had to be pulled by diesel unit, FP7A, No. 200. In a letter to passengers, the association apologized, saying, "Circumstances beyond our control have caused a change in power and itinerary today. Last weekend, steam locomotive No. 1 broke an eccentric rod en route to Spartanburg, South Carolina. The broken end dislodged several staybolts in the boiler. Repairs under way were originally expected to be completed in time to operate No. 1 today. Unfortunately, necessary parts being made will not be finished until early next week, thus precluding steam power. This only became known Thursday evening, too late to postpone or cancel our trip." Passengers hopeful of a ride behind the famous No.1 did, however, get a little extra bang for the buck as the excursion was extended "all the way to Elkhorn City, Kentucky, some 82 miles farther than originally planned. Trackage north of St. Paul, Virginia, is particularly scenic, and we will concentrate most photo stops in this area. In addition, Clinchfield has added the normally extra-fare air-conditioned observation car, White Oak."

In correspondence for this book, Roger Cook of Oradell, New Jersey, said he and his wife, Chi, were aboard the June 21 excursion. Since it was their fourth of five Clinchfield excursions, Cook said he was not disappointed but, rather, "thrilled to learn we would be going all the way to Elkhorn City, especially since lots of photo stops were planned." The Cooks were

The June 14, 1975 food-poisoning incident was magnified when the Clinchfield No. 1 broke down. The steam engine was still undergoing repairs a week later, so Clinchfield 200, a diesel, replaced the No. 1 for the June 21, 1975 excursion. *Photo by Roger Cook.*

also treated to two parlor seats in the White Oak. So, it would seem that much unhappiness from the previous week led, in a very roundabout way, to a happy occasion for at least two passengers the following week.

13

HOWARD BAKER AND POLITICAL POWER ABOARD THE NO. 1

The Clinchfield No. 1 wasn't the most powerful engine on the rails, but for a few days in the 1970s, it was a powerhouse of politics, carrying the weight of political ambition on well-worn train tracks across Tennessee. Indeed, there were times when it attracted some of the most powerful people in Tennessee—and even Washington, D.C.—to its side.

The most famous was U.S. senator Howard Baker Jr., who hired the Clinchfield Railroad's increasingly media-friendly excursion services for a whistle-stop campaign across Tennessee "from Bristol to Memphis" in 1972, a feat he repeated in 1978.

By becoming, in 1966, the first elected Republican senator from Tennessee since Reconstruction, Baker became a rising star in the Grand Old Party and was briefly considered by President Richard Nixon, in 1971, to fill an open seat on the Supreme Court (William Rehnquist got the nod instead).

In 1972, Baker was seeking reelection, but he faced a formidable opponent in three-term U.S. representative Ray Blanton. While politicians had used whistle-stop campaigns for many years, the 1970s were giving way to modern times. Still, nostalgia plays big in politics, and Baker used this to his advantage, drawing large crowds to hear his speeches delivered from the back of a passenger train pulled by a vintage steam engine.

Dubbed the "Baker Special" for these sojourns, the Clinchfield No. 1 pulled its campaign excursion from the mountains of northeast Tennessee in Bristol to the city of Memphis—a four-day haul that included twenty-six stops to greet voters. A 1978 poster shows a hand-

The Baker Special in Nashville in 1978. U.S. senator Howard Baker Jr. twice used the No. 1 to lead his whistle-stop campaigns. *Photo by Howard J. Wayt, Courtesy of the Kyle Korienek Collection.*

drawn No. 1 bouncing over hills with the words "All Aboard the Baker Special" prominently at the top. The No. 1's coal tender warmly displays "Clinchfield Rosebud."

"It was like traveling through people's backyards, riding the train," recalled U.S. senator Lamar Alexander in a 2014 interview. Alexander was aboard both Baker Specials in 1972 and 1978, the latter as part of his own successful campaign for governor of Tennessee. "Normally, when you're campaigning, it's through highways cluttered with stores and billboards. But with the train, you're traveling through people's backyards, so you see their wash hanging up, see them sitting on their porches and they're waving at you. It's a great way to see people. It's a terrific way to campaign."

For Alexander, the Baker Special gave the up-and-coming Republican a chance to shine, both as political aide and later as a candidate himself. Like Baker, Alexander would later seek the Republican nomination for president. Both would lead successful statewide campaigns. Alexander would, in 1978, win his first of two terms as governor before winning his U.S. Senate seat in 2002. Baker would win both his 1972 and 1978 campaigns and would later become President Ronald Reagan's chief of staff in 1987 and 1988 and ambassador to Japan from 2001 until 2005.

Baker's special excursions put into focus several political futures and friendships. "I was on both Baker Specials," Alexander said.

I had gone to Washington in 1967 as Senator Baker's legislative assistant when he was first elected and came back to Nashville in 1969 and was practicing law there. I helped Senator Baker recruit some of the campaign workers for his 1972 campaign, including Fred Thompson (actor, future U.S. senator and another candidate for the Republican nomination for president) to be the Middle Tennessee campaign chairman…I met some good friends on the Baker Special. One of them was a youngster named Sandy Beall. Sandy had dropped out of the University of Tennessee and had opened a restaurant called Ruby Tuesday, and he later grew that restaurant to a chain of more than eight hundred restaurants around the world and he's the CEO now…He became one of my best friends. I met him on the train, and because of that we've been friends ever since. I would have been thirty-two, and he would have been twenty-two. He was from Knoxville, and he knew the Baker family. He was interested in politics. At the time, he probably had only one restaurant, maybe two.

The future, too, seemed set for Alexander's young son, Drew, aboard the Baker Special. Drew now serves as director of publishing for music powerhouse Curb Records in Nashville, Tennessee. The Baker Special attracted several of country's biggest stars, including comedian and singer Ray Stevens and the legendary Roy Acuff.

"When the Baker Special ran in 1972," Alexander recalled, "I got on it with my young son, Drew, who at that time was three years old. Well, Roy Acuff was on the train, too. We have a picture of Drew sitting on Roy Acuff's lap on the Baker Special, and Drew now has that photo hanging in his office at Curb Records in Nashville."

Acuff changed the lyrics to his famous hit "Wabash Cannonball" to the "Baker Cannonball" for Senator Baker's whistle-stop and would perform the revamped song at stops to the delight of those who turned out to see the senator, its famous passengers and, more often than not, the train itself.

"Roy was from Union County and a Republican," Alexander said, "and he campaigned for Senator Baker and he campaigned for me when I ran for governor in 1974 and 1978. Mainly, he'd appear. Everybody knew him, and everybody enjoyed seeing him."

Baker and Alexander were, undoubtedly, seeking votes from the crowds who showed up at carefully picked stops along the route, but not even U.S. senators were a match for the Clinchfield No. 1's fame. George Hatcher, the engine's fireman, remembered talking to the crowds from the front of the train as much as the senator did stumping from the rear. "When we took

Aboard the 1978 Baker Special, county music legend Roy Acuff chats with Drew
Alexander, son of Lamar Alexander, then a candidate for governor of Tennessee. *Courtesy of
U.S. senator Lamar Alexander.*

Senator Baker," Hatcher recalled, "most of the people would gather around the steam engine, and he'd be at the back of the train. But I don't guess he cared too much about that. All these people came out because the Baker Special was coming to town…The senator got elected both times, so we must have been doing something right."

Politicians, Alexander admitted, often rely on a gimmick to draw the crowd, sometimes with more success than others. "Baker knew that," Alexander said. He continued:

> *By the time we were crossing the state with the Baker Special, passenger trains were gone, so this excursion was something else. I remember my mother was a schoolteacher. She taught nursery school and kindergarten for thirty-five years in Maryville in the '40s, '50s and '60s, and she always took her kindergarten class on a train ride from Knoxville to Lenior City so they could say they'd been on a train. So the Baker Special was a big event. The idea of riding a passenger train was something else. Nobody got to do that anymore, and nobody had seen a passenger train in many years. So to see this special train come through loaded with people was a big event, and that's what drew the crowds.*
>
> *But that's politics. Politicians are used to drawing crowds. In 1948, Congressman [B. Carroll] Reese from the First Judicial District wanted to be the U.S. senator, so he got Roy Acuff to run for governor, who was very popular after World War II, so that Roy could draw the crowd, he and the Smoky Mountain Boys. I met someone in Cookeville that said Roy drew a crowd of 30,000 people, and when they were done playing, Roy made a short speech. He would then introduce Mr. Reese, but the only problem was that as soon as Roy got down and Congressman Reese starting speaking, everybody left. Roy got more votes for governor than Congressman Reese got for senator. So politicians are used to using things to draw a crowd, and having a passenger train run through backyards is a very good way to do it.*

Clinchfield Railroad paperwork at the Archives of Appalachia details what a significant undertaking the statewide excursion was. It involved coordination with three other railroads: the Southern, Louisville & Nashville and the Illinois Central Gulf.

On October 20, 1978, J.L. Lonon spelled out the train's itinerary: "To protect Special Passenger Train, Bristol, Tennessee, to Memphis, Tennessee…please arrange for movement and delivery to Southern Rail Ry. at Johnson City, Tennessee: Steam Locomotive No. 1, Diesel Units 250–869,

This postcard was given out by U.S. senator Howard Baker on his 1972 whistle-stop campaign swing across Tennessee behind the Clinchfield No. 1. *Courtesy of the Dan Garland Collection.*

Car 114 (observation end north), Coaches 110–111, and Tupelo River (Sou. Ry. pullman car), in that order from head end, Erwin to Johnson City."

Lonon detailed that the train was to leave Erwin at 5:00 a.m. Monday, October 30, with "the entire train expected to be returned to Johnson City via Carnegie interchange late evening, November 3, 1978, for immediate movement to Erwin." During the four-day excursion, Clinchfield Railroad personnel had reservations at the Hyatt Regency in Knoxville on October 30, at the Choo-Choo Hilton in Chattanooga on October 31 and the Sheraton in Nashville on November 1. Hotel rooms were reserved for the Hatcher brothers, fireman George and engineer Ed, as well as Bob Lusby, P.O. Likens, Milburn Rice, David Crockett, Malone Peterson, Bob White and Everette Allen. Pullman accommodations aboard coaches were also detailed for railroad personnel with rooms and "roomettes" already assigned.

Precautions were even taken to ensure enough fresh personnel would be available halfway through the trip, as Ed Hatcher was undergoing cancer treatment in 1978 and was often ill. Reservations were made for engineers R.W. Hatcher Sr. and J.L. Davis Jr. to leave Tri-Cities Airport in Blountville, Tennessee, aboard a Southern Air Line flight departing 12:55 p.m. and arriving in Nashville at 1:01 p.m., where they were instructed to take an airport limousine or taxi to Sheraton Hotel.

In a letter to J.I. Adams, assistant vice-president for the Louisville & Nashville Railroad in Kentucky, Lonon wrote, "It is very important this train be given the most expeditious handling…The Clinchfield will have sufficient qualified steam locomotive personnel on train to keep it operating continuously on return trip, Memphis to Erwin, to assist your crews." The railroad personnel took the train across the state in four days and were to return the train to Erwin in just one day on November 3. The campaign events were done, so stops were not an issue. But the old train was pushed hard to get back to Erwin for a previously chartered excursion on November 4, 1978.

R.F. Lusby outlined the schedule, again in documents stored at the Archives of Appalachia. The train would officially begin its whistle-stop campaign in Bristol, leaving at 9:00 a.m. on October 30. The remaining stops that day were Johnson City, 9:50 a.m.; Greeneville, 11:20 a.m.; Bulls Gap, 12:20 p.m.; Morristown, 1:25 p.m.; Jefferson City, 2:25 p.m.; and Knoxville, 4:00 p.m. On October 31, the train left Knoxville at 8:30 a.m. with stops in Lenoir City at 9:15 a.m., Loudon at 9:50 a.m., Sweetwater at 10:25 a.m., Athens at 11:15 a.m., Cleveland at 12:25 p.m., Ooltewah at 1:25 p.m. and Chattanooga at 2:10 p.m. On November 1, the day would begin again in Chattanooga at 9:00 a.m., followed by Cowan at 10:00 a.m., Tullahoma at 10:45 a.m., Wartrace at 11:35 a.m., Murfreesboro at 12:35 p.m., Smyrna at 1:15 p.m. and Nashville at 2:30 p.m. The final day, November 2, would see a start from the state capital at 7:00 a.m. and stops in Dickson at 8:10 a.m., Lexington at 11:30 a.m., Jackson at 12:40 p.m., Brownsville, 3:50 p.m. and, finally, Memphis at 6:00 p.m.

J. Lee Annis Jr. detailed the significance of the Baker Special in his book, *Howard Baker: Conciliator in an Age of Crisis*, when he wrote:

> *While confident, Baker took nothing for granted. Ten days before the [1972] election, he launched a whistle-stop tour on a ninety-year-old locomotive once used to rescue victims of the Johnstown flood. Redubbed the "Baker Cannonball" by Roy Acuff, the Rosebud was met by large crowds at every stop. Each audience was treated to a set by Acuff and other country stars before Baker would appear and link his fortunes to those of Richard Nixon, who[m] he said was ending the Vietnam War and keeping inflation to a minimum. Baker exhibited his good nature on many occasions, but most tellingly when he spotted Mrs. Maybelle G. Clement, the late governor's mother, waving from the Dickson hotel, where*

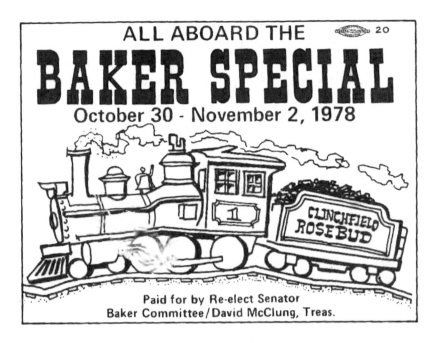

Promotional item used for the 1978 Baker Special. *Courtesy of the Dan Garland Collection.*

During his 1972 campaign, Senator Howard Baker Jr. is flanked by George Hatcher and Ed Hatcher in the cab of the Clinchfield No. 1. *Courtesy of Martha Erwin/Clinchfield Railroad Museum.*

her son had been born. Baker praised the memory of his 1966 opponent, a man he considered a friend, and recalled that he had never had to set the record straight with Clement as he had to do many times with [his current opponent, Ray] *Blanton. When the Rosebud reached Memphis, Baker heralded "the dawn of a new day in Tennessee electoral history." Tennessee gave him 716,534 votes, more than they had ever before given any candidate for office, to Blanton's 440,599.*

Baker, exhausted at the end of the 1972 whistle-stop campaign, spoke with the Associated Press for a story with the headline "Rosebud's One-Time Lady for Baker." The senator said, "Not only do I not have any plans for using a train in the future, I don't have any plans of having a campaign in the future." He said, "It's sort of like asking a lady right after she has had a baby if she wants another." Of course, he would campaign again, and he would engage the Baker Special once more, six years later.

When asked how he felt about the Clinchfield No. 1's special excursion in his name, the senator said, "My brains are still jostled. I have a great affection for 'Rosebud.' She's a great lady...She pulled that train across the state with great success and without a breakdown."

By the end of 1972, the term "dirty tricks" had steadfastly entered the American political lexicon. It is most closely connected to the Watergate scandal during President Richard Nixon's time in office, in which, famously, Baker, serving as vice-chairman of a Senate committee investigating the Watergate scandal asked, "What did the president know, and when did he know it?" During the 1970s, Tennessee was particularly scandalized by "dirty politics," and one incident was so daring, it threatened to not only derail a campaign but also a campaign train, specifically the Clinchfield No. 1. And in the mix was Baker's 1972 opponent, Ray Blanton.

Blanton, elected governor in 1974, oversaw an administration mired in scandal and would, after leaving the governor's mansion, serve a prison term for mail fraud and other offenses. Three years after the first Baker Special in 1972, Tennessee media began reporting the shocking details of a plot to cripple the No. 1 as it carried Baker across the state.

A May 3, 1975 report by the Associated Press details an alleged plot by Blanton aides to halt the Clinchfield No. 1 on the tracks. Under the headline "Blanton Aide 'Admits' to Tricks Talk," the AP outlines a story from the *Memphis Press-Scimitar* that claims Blanton aide Phillip Mattingly admitted he "took part in discussions about sabotage against Baker's train" three years earlier. Mattingly, according to the *Press-Scimitar*, claimed that "almost all of the conversation about dirty tricks came from James A. Brown Jr.," an advance man for Blanton in 1972.

Brown, according to the *Press-Scimitar* and the AP reports, claimed the Blanton campaign "was marked by...underhanded plots against Baker" in which Blanton workers "planned to slow the Baker train by greasing rails on a hillside, spreading the tracks or planting signal flares ordering the train to stop."

"The purpose," the AP reported, "was to slow the train and leave waiting crowds at stops ahead antagonized." The sneaky plan was a testament, at least, to the crowd-drawing power of the popular Clinchfield No. 1 and its nostalgic passenger train. The published reports claimed Mattingly, long after Blanton was defeated by Baker, "openly bragged about the sabotage plans." It was reported that the FBI and the Justice Department launched an investigation, but there's no indication any charges were ever brought.

Alexander recalled that the plot was known to those aboard the train, but perhaps it was so outlandish, few took it seriously. "It was sort of a dirty tricks rumor," the senator said in 2014.

> There was a rumor that Blanton was going to put oil on the tracks and slow the train down. We think that was more than a rumor, and it was certainly a big rumor...Political dirty tricks were in the news a few years later because of President Nixon...and it was after that that people said maybe Baker himself was a potential victim of dirty politics...At the time, I don't think we were very worried about it. It was just part of the political gossip at the time, but it certainly made the ride more interesting.

In the end, the Baker Special seemed to resonate with the public and, Alexander said, had at least some influence with voters. In 1978, with Alexander facing opposition for governor from charismatic Knoxville businessman Jake Butcher, the Republican needed all the help he could get. "It had been a real tough campaign," he recalled.

> I was running against Jake Butcher, and Senator Baker was running his own campaign, as I was. But then he invited me to join him on the train, and that was wonderful because we sort of shared each other's momentum as the train drove across the state in the last few days of the campaign. It was a real boost to my campaign...It added momentum to a winning campaign and was a very big help.

Nostalgia, as always with the Clinchfield No. 1, was a winner with the public.

Alexander's grandfather Reu Raymond Rankin was a railroad man. While aboard the Baker Special, Alexander carried a special memento. "My grandfather…was called R.R. Rankin; Railroad Rankin, I would call him," Alexander said. "And he had a big old watch, a pocket watch. It was very important for trains to be on time, so railroaders carried pocket watches. He gave me his pocket watch when he died, and I carried that pocket watch during my campaign in 1978 and aboard the Baker Special."

For Baker, Alexander and the Clinchfield No. 1, it seemed that time was, indeed, on their side.

14

NOT SO "SPECIAL": SANTA CLAUS SUED

The Clinchfield No. 1's first public performance was to pull the railroad's famed Santa Train in 1968, and the locomotive—and its famous namesake passenger—annually received praise far and wide, regularly garnering national media coverage highlighting the railroad's philanthropic endeavor. So it came as a surprise in 1974—and with its own share of headlines—when a Virginia woman filed a $30,000 lawsuit against the Clinchfield, the Kingsport Chamber of Commerce and even Santa Claus himself. For a time, the suit threatened to derail the annual holiday spectacular that had been a tradition since 1943.

The Santa Train, described in 1974 by the *Kingsport Times-News* as "the annual journey of the 'Jolly Ol Elf' from Elkhorn City, Kentucky, to Kingsport on Clinchfield Railroad Company's Old Engine Number 1," has over the years delivered so many gifts of food, clothing, school supplies and toys that it routinely is described not in the number of gifts but by their weight in tonnage. For many years, those gifts were tossed from the back of the train to waiting crowds in the coalfields of Virginia and Kentucky.

The importance of the Santa Train—and the novelty of Santa being named in a lawsuit, no doubt—made Denna G. Darnell's lawsuit the top story in the December 19, 1974 issue of the *Kingsport Times-News*, relegating "Rockefeller Becomes Vice President Today" to only slightly above the fold. The lead headline was "Woman Wants $30,000 from Santa—Claims Eye Injury in Scott Lawsuit." Darnell, of Fort Blackmore, claimed she was struck in the eye by books thrown from the train as she waited with her grandchildren at Hill Station to see Santa.

The Santa Train earned the No. 1 widespread media attention. Clinchfield general manager T.D. Moore, seen here directly above the word Santa in the banner, bends down for a handful of candy to toss to eager youngsters. *Photo by David DeVault.*

The original filing on December 16, 1974, in Scott County, Virginia, Circuit Court petitioned Judge Joseph N. Cridlin to render judgment for personal injuries. "Santa's address," the Kingsport newspaper wrote, is listed in care of the Kingsport Chamber of Commerce and alleges:

> *The defendant, Kingsport Chamber of Commerce, anticipating that the season had arrived when children's fantasy and imagination soared, turning to the joys of Christmas…agreed and covenanted with the defendant, Clinchfield Railroad Company, to undertake a joint enterprise to transport the Grand Old Man, Santa Claus, by train to bring joy and cheer to all along the rail route…* [Chamber officials], *influenced by eleemosynary motives, retained Santa Claus and his elves to ride Olde Engine No. 1 of Clinchfield.*

The suit described the incident this way:

> *At approximately 12 noon, as Olde Engine No. 1 proceeded through Scott County, Virginia, your plaintiff, who is a loving and compassionate*

At the end of downtown, the Clinchfield No. 1 can be seen as it pulls the Santa Train on the outskirts of St. Paul, Virginia, in 1968. *Photo by David DeVault.*

grandmother but not in good health because of heart trouble, accompanied her two excited grandchildren to Hill Station along side the Clinchfield Railroad tracks to anxiously await the grand arrival of Santa, and soon thereafter as everyone nervously awaited the appearance of Santa, Olde No. 1 came chugging down the tracks to the joy and thrill of all, drawing ever nearer to your plaintiff and two grandchildren, and as Santa's car approached…

At this point, Darnell's attorney, S.W. Coleman III, left behind his legalese and launched into a less-than-eleemosynary rewrite of Clement C. Moore's famous "'Twas the Night Before Christmas":

Lo and behold! What should appear
One of Santa's helpers, not of good cheer,
The trip had been long, tiring and slow,
Santa's little elf had no rosy glow,
The toys he hurled like a dagger or spear,
Wreaking havoc, anger and occasional fear,
He drew back his right and three books he let fly,
Cutting and damaging your plaintiff's left eye.
She was hurled to the ground in a heap and a lump,
With brilliant red blood from the cut and the bump,
Unconscious she lay while the children did run,

Granny lay stricken, what had Santa done?
With help from afar Granny finally came to,
To the hospital she flew to see what the matter,
With stars in her head and great deal of clatter.

With that, Coleman returned to his case, demanding "with some hesitancy as Christmas Day approaches for fear that your plaintiff may suffer further reprisals" for judgment against each defendant.

The defendants' response in the case of *Denna G. Darnell v. Santa Claus, et al* was to deny the allegations, refuse to admit guilt of "any careless or negligent act" and call for "strict proof" of Darnell's alleged injuries.

Not to be outdone by Coleman's literary license, Charles B. Flannagan II, counsel for the Kingsport Chamber, penned his own take on the famous Christmas poem, which he presented to the court:

'Twas a few days before Christmas
when old Santa did appear,
To spread Christmas joy
to those who were near.
Children ran to the tracks
to see something uncanny,
For there they were met by
crotchety old Granny.
As the children excitedly
lunged for their gifts,
Old Granny decided
she would assume the risks.
The children did shout
and jump and scream,
But Granny stood fast
as though in a dream.
Without giving a thought
to protecting herself,
Granny suffered misfortune
and now blames the elf.
And so to her plea
that money we should lose,
We offer to send switches
to fill Granny's shoes.

On the Santa Train's return, folks posed with the newly remade Clinchfield No. 1. Santa had detrained and can be seen in the background atop a firetruck. *Photo by David DeVault.*

While attorneys on both sides seemed to be taking some jolly pleasure in their court documents, the Clinchfield Railroad was not inclined to be so flip about a $30,000 lawsuit. In a letter sent to the corporate office in New York City and addressed to Frank C. Puleo, secretary for the Carolina, Clinchfield and Ohio Railway, attorney Bradley Roberts wrote:

> *One of the attorneys who represents Kingsport Chamber of Commerce is the same calibre poet as is plaintiff's attorney. For your information and edification, I enclose a copy of the grounds of defense filed on behalf of the Kingsport Chamber of Commerce. The attorney (Flannagan) stated the poetic portion of his pleading was published in the Kingsport, Tennessee, newspaper and he immediately got a call from the secretary of the Chamber of Commerce in Kingsport who was very much agitated that the Chamber's pleading referred to the plaintiff as a "crotchety old Granny."*

The Clinchfield's local attorneys, the law officers of Stant and Roberts and Quillen and Carter, were in full gear to stop the suit and to prove the railroad simply operated the train and was not in a "joint enterprise" with the chamber.

In a December 23, 1974 letter to attorney Cecil D. Quillen, Robert F. Sams, assistant to the general counsel for the Clinchfield in Erwin, wrote, "Will you see that the Clinchfield Railroad Company's interest is protected to the fullest? Also I believe Mr. Moore, our general manager, would like for you to cause Mr. Coleman as much trouble as possible with this suit."

By the first week of February 1975, Darnell's attorney had amended the suit to exclude Santa Claus with the *Kingsport Times-News* reporting, "Santa Claus no longer has to defend himself in Scott County." The chamber and Clinchfield Railroad remained defendants, and the railroad continued efforts to crush Darnell's suit. In a letter dated February 12, 1975, Sams once again wrote to Quillen, this time with information he claimed would show the elderly woman's injuries were not severe. "I have learned from Mr. Ted Stultz, assistant to the superintendent in Kingsport, that Dr. Mickey Shull has discussed the injury to Mrs. Darnell with a doctor in the Nicklesville, Virginia, clinic; and, according to Dr. Shull, her injuries are not as serious as she contended in her complaint. This may be useful to use in the development of the defense."

Fighting the charges, the railroad claimed it never entered into a joint enterprise with the chamber other than "to furnish transportation" and that, in fact, it was Darnell who was to blame for her injuries, as she "did not exercise proper care for her own safety." With a nod to the previous court filings, the railroad's attorney declined to wax poetic, telling the court, the Clinchfield "does not consider it necessary to write a poetic response to the amended judgment, inasmuch as Santa Claus has now been nonsuited as to this action."

Lawyers continued talking and filing motions until the summer when, finally, an agreement was reached among all parties. In a June 27, 1975 article, the *Kingsport Times-News* wrote, "Clinchfield general manager T.D. Moore said each defendant...paid Mrs. Darnell $635 in the settlement," far below the $30,000 she originally sought. While the railroad had fought its inclusion in the suit under the pretense that it was simply a vehicle, Moore, with the lawsuit behind him, wasn't content in merely being part of the hired help, making it clear that the railroad spent considerable money to be part of the annual holiday festivities and warning that lawsuits in the future would put an end to the Clinchfield's involvement.

"We take action reluctantly," Moore told the newspaper,

> *because it was a question of whether it might affect future running of the train, or might set a precedent that would result in the Christmas train*

Ron Flanary captured the Clinchfield No. 1's Santa Train in this beautiful painting that was made into a popular print. *Courtesy of Ron Flanary.*

The 1977 Santa Train steams through Fort Blackmore, Virginia, delivering gifts and Christmas goodwill to residents waiting along the tracks. *Courtesy of the Ron Flanary Collection.*

being stopped. Although running the Christmas train from Elkhorn City, Kentucky, to Kingsport is the highlight of the season for me, it has become increasingly expensive. It presently costs the railroad about $5,000 a year, and we seriously thought of stopping the train after the suit was filed.

And at that point, Moore drew a line in the sand, telling the newspaper the 1975 Santa Train would go on as planned, but if any suits were filed, it would end the train's long run.

The Santa Train is still running every holiday season, but it is likely there may be more lawyers aboard than elves.

15

EXTRA-SPECIAL CLINCHFIELD:
TO THE OCEAN AND DOWN TO FLORIDA

By the mid-1970s, the Clinchfield No. 1's excursions were commonplace from Tennessee to Virginia, Kentucky and North Carolina and back and forth from Spartanburg, South Carolina, but the trips had, with the exception of the 1972 whistle-stop campaign across Tennessee for U.S. senator Howard Baker Jr., stayed mostly on the tracks of the Clinchfield Railroad. But 1978—the last full year of operations for the Clinchfield No. 1 and its celebrated excursions—would find "Rosebud" pushing far beyond the boundaries of the coal-hauling Clinchfield. Senator Baker used the train again for his reelection campaign in 1978, but well before the November elections, the No. 1 set out on two of its most extensive excursions—the first, in May, to the coast of South Carolina, and the second, in July, to Tampa, Florida.

The May special took ol' No. 1 all the way to the quaint and historic Atlantic Ocean coastal area of Georgetown County, South Carolina, located between Charleston and Myrtle Beach. It was a nearly seven-hundred-mile round trip for the historic locomotive and one celebrated throughout the Carolina Lowcountry. Local officials estimated that thousands came out to see the historic steam engine, the first back in the area in decades, and many hoped to earn a ride behind the No. 1 on several short excursions offered to the public. In one of several effusive articles detailing every turn of the No. 1's ten wheels, the *Georgetown Times* wrote, "The Clinchfield Special…gave rides to roughly 5,000 people with some finding out the odds were something like going to Heaven—some would make it and some wouldn't—but only a few of the latter."

The No. 1 made a special visit to South Carolina's Lowcountry in May 1978. Al Rogers, an Andrews resident and engineer for Seaboard Coastline, and young Kerri Barrineau pose in the cab. *Courtesy of the Sandra M. Epps and Micah Epps Collection.*

Family Lines executive and Andrews native Ettre Vee Rogers McDonald was responsible for bringing the Clinchfield No. 1 to Georgetown County. To her right is Charles W. Cagle. *Photo by Mary A. Cagle.*

The train was the star of Andrews Good Ole Days, dubbed by the *Times* as "a most effervescent part of the Georgetown County Lowland Fling." Andrews is a railroad town similar to Erwin, Tennessee, home of the Clinchfield No. 1, and many old-time railroaders showed up to relive the past as the Clinchfield No. 1 rolled into town. Not since President Franklin Roosevelt rode a train into Andrews in 1944 on his way to visit Bernard Baruch at his Hobcaw Plantation had a train's arrival been as anticipated as the No. 1's. Benjamin Brown, a local man who started working for the railroad the same year Roosevelt came to town, recalled that the president's train was the largest ever to ride the rails in Andrews. "He came through on the Orange Blossom Special and stopped at the station," Brown said. "Did he talk? Well he stuck his head out and nodded." The *Times* promised the No. 1's arrival would "bring back many memories to those men who worked with the railroad during its heyday, as well as the Andrews town folk who 'remember when.'"

Clinchfield's reliable old steam engine, dubbed by the *Times* as "a unique Cinderella of a train," didn't disappoint. The train's arrival in Georgetown County was credited to Eleanor Moody, who, in planning for the event, seized upon Andrews's past as a train town, and prominent Georgetown attorney James B. Moore, who in turn contacted Ettre Vee Rogers McDonald, the assistant vice-president of the Family Lines Systems, headquartered in Jacksonville, Florida, and parent company of the Clinchfield. McDonald, rare at the time as a female railroad executive, was a native of Andrews. She immediately contacted T.D. Moore at the Clinchfield to bring his favorite little train to the coastal celebration. She arrived for the event aboard the train in period costume with as many local, regional and state politicians as the Hatcher brothers' train could haul, among them Richard Riley, candidate for governor. Riley would go on to win that election and serve two terms, and in 1993, he was appointed secretary of education by President Bill Clinton, who considered Riley for Supreme Court justice before opting for Ruth Bader Ginsburg. The No. 1, it would seem, always provided a winning edge for politicians.

In announcing the No. 1's arrival several weeks before the Lowland Fling, the *Times*—in an article headlined "Clinchfield's No. 1 to Chug Here"—wrote, "The train that's coming to Andrews is…like a chameleon. It is a happy little train that, when it appears as a mainline attraction in the mountains of Virginia, bears the name of 'The Clinchfield Santa Claus Special.' And when it serves the run from Spartanburg to the Blue Ridge Mountains, it is 'The Clinchfield Special.' And when it comes to

More than five thousand people took rides behind the Clinchfield No. 1 when the locomotive brought an excursion train to South Carolina's Lowcountry in 1978. Dozens watch as the No. 1 arrives in Andrews. *Photo by Mary A. Cagle.*

Andrews with a carefully planned schedule lined up for three days of delighting the kids and grown-ups, it's going to add a new name. It's going to be called 'The Lowland Fling Special.'" (It should be noted, however, that in articles covering the train's arrival in Georgetown, it was most often referred to as the Clinchfield Special.) According to another article by Ethlyn Missroon in March 9, 1978, the response to bring the No. 1 to the Lowcountry "was immediate and enthusiastic." The *Times* described the No. 1's regular route through the Blue Ridge Mountains as "an incomparable scenic route—unless one were to think to the Lowcountry and its marshes, seascapes and gentle breezes blowing sea oats."

According to the *Times*, McDonald boarded the Clinchfield No. 1 in Charleston on Thursday, May 4, as the train made its way toward Georgetown County and Andrews, arriving at 4:00 p.m. with McDonald and T.D. Moore aboard. Several opportunities for the public to ride were set for Friday and Saturday, May 5 and 6, at 9:30 and 11:45 a.m. and 2:00 p.m. and again on Sunday, May 7, at 1:00 p.m., when Riley and many other dignitaries were welcomed aboard.

When the train arrived in Andrews, according to the *Times*, it "found folks waiting at the old depot site just as they did around the turn of the century. The primely polished-silver countenanced little engine, the darling of the Clinchfield Family Lines train people," arrived right on the dot. The newspaper said each ride averaged 650 passengers, and one took as many as 721, with crowds anxiously awaiting a chance to board. One child was overheard to whisper to his mother about approaching rain clouds by saying, "Suppose it rains. We can't ride!" His mind was eased when he was told that the Clinchfield No. 1 pulled a "real train" and that "this train has a top... it's not like the Six Flags one." Several youngsters were also allowed into the cab, where they were shown the ropes by the Hatcher brothers.

The newspaper said a railroad spokesman

hesitated to estimate how many tons of coal it required to keep the Clinchfield Special chugging. At least one coal car of the black jewels was shoveled into the train's hungry fire box and the end result for all to see and smell was a constant stream of heavy black smoke from the stack. One old trainman, smelling the acrid cinder-flavored fumes murmured wistfully, "They sure took the heart out of railroading when they got rid of the smoke." At night, after a long hard day, the little Clinchfield engine was berthed at a siding next to U.S. Highway 521 within the city limits of Andrews. As she sat there quietly snuffling to herself, it was a common sight to see a lone person or perhaps two or three standing there in the darkness, arms folded, listening to sounds long gone and now surprisingly come back for a short while.

In summing up the event, the *Times* wrote:

In the back of everyone's mind was awareness of the incredible generosity of the Seaboard Coastline Railroad and the Family Lines System. The operation of the train, the man-hours of those who courteously met and dealt with the crowds, ran the engines and ensured safety represent investments upon which no price could be placed. It was history relived and Georgetown County at large and Andrews, in particular, are indebted to the train complex and those who promoted her appearance, especially a vivacious one-time Andrews girl, Ettre Vee Rogers McDonald. She left Sunday afternoon after riding a final time—and, understandably, left her voice in Andrews, a victim of much talking and greeting. But, she said, the experience was one of the most wonderful of her entire life and she felt that anything she could say would be inadequate. Not too surprisingly, many of

The bimonthly company magazine *Family Lines* featured the Clinchfield No. 1's "Tampa Turn" for its September/October 1978 cover story, comparing the 2,200-mile trip to "time travel." *Courtesy of Martha Erwin/Clinchfield Railroad Museum.*

*those who benefited through the generosity of the Clinchfield Family Lines,
found themselves in quite the same position; they just couldn't say enough.*

In a May 11 follow-up story in the *Times*, chamber president Tad Fogel said he
was "ecstatic" over the success of the Lowland Fling, "particularly the all-out
interest shown by all age groups in the Clinchfield Special."

A little more than two months after the successful trip to South Carolina's
Lowcountry, the Clinchfield No. 1 would set out on its most extensive excursion
ever: a 2,231-mile, fifteen-day, six-state round-trip from Erwin, Tennessee, to
Tampa, Florida, and back, known simply as "the Tampa Run" or "the Tampa
Turn." Many years ago, Moore might have had trouble convincing railroad
executives with the Clinchfield's parent company, the Family Lines System,
that the refurbished No. 1 could be a public relations boon for the railroad, but
by 1978, it was clear he was right all along. And Family Lines executives were
eager to capture some of it for the corporation and not just the Clinchfield.
In the September/October issue of the company magazine, *Family Lines*, the
cover story featured the little Tennessee locomotive in a story titled "Our
Florida 'Time Machine' Delights Thousands." And that it did—with stops in
more than three dozen towns and cities in South Carolina, Georgia, Florida
and Alabama before returning home and having transported 6,945 passengers.
The star destination of Tampa hosted several official events, including the
city's ninety-first birthday celebration and a reenactment of Teddy Roosevelt's
Army Rough Riders' arrival during the Spanish-American War. A press
release announced it was an "opportunity to once again see a near vanished
breed of Americana Railroadiana, a steam engine with a passenger train."
The release even noted the diesel helpers, noting the F-7B units were "early
diesels…and getting to be a rare breed" themselves.

Clearly pleased with the results, the *Family Lines* magazine could barely
contain its enthusiasm, writing:

> *They began gathering half an hour before the arrival, youngsters barely
> able to remember yesterday, and others with keen recollections of rail trips
> in pre-jet and super highway years…*
>
> *Presently a wisp of black smoke appeared, far down the tracks, and a
> headlight shown…*
>
> *"Here it comes! Here it comes!," the children cried as they jumped to
> their feet. Amid a swirl of coal smoke, steam and dust, the old engine
> and its train rolled grandly to a stop beside the station. News cameras
> whirred, and pens of reporters scribbled. The crowds "ooh'd" and "ah'd"*

The No. 1 moves down Polk Street and into downtown Tampa, Florida, on July 22, 1978, as part of the city's ninety-first birthday celebration and Rough Riders Day. *Photo by Fred Clark Jr.*

Festivities in Tampa ranged from nostalgic (the No. 1) and historic (Rough Riders) to contemporary and revealing (the Tampa Bay Buccaneers' cheerleaders, aptly named SwashBucklers). *Photo by Fred Clark Jr.*

the machine before them, from its tall driving wheels to its (silver) boiler front and straight smoke stack as one of its handlers dropped to the ground to administer oil to rods and motion work. This scene was repeated over and over again, at scores of Florida-served communities during late July, when Family Lines' ninety-six-year-old steam locomotive, Old Number One, again took to the rails on a tour through the Southland. And, for two weeks, the venerable engine became indeed our "Time Machine" to the past!

While the crowds were certainly enthralled, planning for the trip began weeks before and was probably more tedious and laborious than enthralling. Correspondence between railroad officials and the crew were detailed. In one, four items of general information were outlined:

1) A clothes rod has been provided in concession room of Car 106 for garment bags and clothing.
2) Credit has been established at each motel for rooms and meals.
3) Arrangements have been made at each overnight stop to clean and water coaches and locomotive. Thirty-eight tons of coal in CRR 16227 (gondola) has been sent ahead.
4) Transportation will be provided from train to motel and return.

Arrival and departure times for each of the nearly four dozen stops—from a 12:01 p.m. departure from Erwin, Tennessee, on July 18—were meticulously arranged, which was important since, as a Seaboard Coast Line press release noted, "this will be the first time in many years that a steam locomotive has operated on SCL tracks." Once off the Clinchfield's regular route in Spartanburg, South Carolina, the No. 1 had to travel on the freight-line tracks of several railroads to make its varied destinations, all of which required detailed planning. As early as May 25, assistant chief dispatcher J.F. Garner was writing to W.I. Smith Jr., the chief dispatcher in Savannah, saying, "Re: Operation of Clinchfield Steam Train, CRR No. 1, 2 B-units and 10 cars via Savannah Division July 19th and 20th, I know of no operational difficulties that may be envisioned but herewith some ideas that may enhance the operation and prevent some difficulties from arising." With that, Garner outlined nearly a dozen "ideas," including instructions that it

will be necessary to oil steam engine CRR No. 1 every 35-50 miles…12 blocks of ice for Parlor Car White Oak…1 engineman-watchman to watch No. 1 (and) keep up fire properly…preferably someone, if available, who is familiar with steam engines....Suggest engine will be serviced along with White Oak, and parked where the public can view No. 1 and the press may make pictures along with TV, and where will be away from operations, so no one would get hurt or be wandering around our facilities.

In a letter dated July 7 to G.M. McNeill, superintendent of SCL, Bob Likens detailed the sixteen stops in South Carolina and Georgia on July 19 and assured McNeill that his request for a short complimentary trip for South Carolina representative Jennings G. McAbee and sons would be arranged. Along the entire trip, Bob Likens made detailed notes on the train's progress, noting the number of passengers and whether an arrival or departure time had changed from the original schedule, such as a "1 hr 20 min delay brake test," which he noted on July 28 in Pensacola, Florida. All in all, the No. 1 and its two dedicated diesel units would pull thirteen passenger cars for the trip, including the White Oak.

The schedule for the Tampa Turn was set as such (with various short runs at some stops, including, for example, to Busch Gardens from Tampa):

> *Tuesday, July 18: Erwin, Tennessee, to Spartanburg, South Carolina, 141 miles*
>
> *Wednesday, July 19: Spartanburg, South Carolina, to Savannah, Georgia, 256 miles*
>
> *Thursday, July 20: Savannah, Georgia, to Sanford, Florida, 263 miles*
>
> *Friday, July 21: Sanford, Florida, to Tampa, Florida, 114 miles*
>
> *Saturday, July 22: Tampa, Florida, to Busch Gardens (shuttle trips), 24 miles*
>
> *Sunday, July 23: Tampa, Florida, to Brooksville, Florida, and return, 90 miles*
>
> *Monday, July 24: Tampa, Florida, to Baldwin, Florida, 193 miles*
>
> *Tuesday, July 25: Baldwin, Florida, to Chattahoochee, Florida, 189 miles*
>
> *Wednesday, July 26: Chattahoochee, Florida, to Pensacola, Florida, 161 miles*
>
> *Thursday, July 27: Pensacola, Florida, to Bay-Chem and return, 18 miles*
>
> *Friday, July 28: Pensacola, Florida, to Montgomery, Alabama, 162 miles*
>
> *Saturday, July 29: Montgomery, Alabama, to Atlanta, Georgia, 175 miles*
>
> *Sunday, July 30: Atlanta, Georgia, to Augusta, Georgia, 171 miles*
>
> *Monday, July 31: Augusta, Georgia, to Spartanburg, South Carolina, 133 miles*
>
> *Tuesday, August 1: Spartanburg, South Carolina, to Erwin, Tennessee, 141 miles*
>
> *Total: 2,231 miles*

The Clinchfield No. 1 crisscrossed over Florida in July 1978. Here, Cindy Eaton poses with the No. 1 at the Sanford, Florida train station. *Photo by Fred Clark Jr.*

For the railroad, the No. 1's crisscross through the South was a rousing success—in particular, the focal point of the whole fifteen-day trip: the stay in Tampa. "It was all there," declared Panky Snow in an article published on July 23 in the *Tampa Tribune*, "the lonesome whoo-whooee of the steam whistle, the clanging bell, the cinders blowing through the open windows. And the fun. Hundreds of area residents paid $15 a head ($12 for children under 12) for the privilege of riding the nation's oldest operating steam locomotive." In Tampa, the *Family Lines* magazine explained, little No. 1 and train chugged about the Tampa terminals on short trips from Busch Gardens through Ybor City to the waterfront. On July 22, the No. 1 carried the Rough Riders and the SwashBucklers, cheerleaders for the Tampa Bay Buccaneers, into downtown Tampa, where they were met by cheering crowds. The following day, the Tampa Bay chapter of the National Railway Historical Society ran a round-trip excursion trip for more than six hundred people from Tampa to Brooksville. And the *Tribune* highlighted the sights, sounds and feelings, both on and off the train:

> *When the train turned around and headed back to Tampa, everybody settled into a different routine.*
>
> *Chris Roskay and Phyllis Ann Cole played a game called Crazy Eights. They said they had taken the ride to celebrate their first anniversary of going together.*
>
> *Glenn L. Husted of Ledyard, Connecticut, said he wanted his 14-year-old grandson, George Husted, to ride behind a real steam locomotive.*
>
> *"I started as a railroad telegrapher when I was 18, back in 1926," he said. "Later, I worked 18 years with the Southern Pacific."*
>
> *The train had just passed a cheering crowd attending go-cart races at Land O' Lakes when passengers got an added surprise.*
>
> *On one side of the tracks, a teen-ager lay on the ground, dramatically clutching an arrow "protruding" from his chest. At the same time, on the other side of the train, a teen-age girl, dressed as an Indian maid, raced her pinto pony madly though the trees, victoriously waving a bow and arrow overhead.*

But Tampa wasn't the end for the excursion, so after departing, the *Family Lines* magazine wrote, the "Number One and entourage took a more leisurely gait and one with a wider geographic swing. That made possible stops at many intermediate places to give short one-way rides to handicapped children, senior citizens and other special groups." Down to Tampa, the No. 1 had picked up groups at Spartanburg, Woodville, Laurens and Greenwood,

The steam engine from the Appalachian Mountains chugs through Lake Alfred, Florida, and past palm trees and underneath live oaks naturally adorned with Spanish moss. *Photo by Fred Clark Jr.*

South Carolina; Augusta and Savannah, Georgia; and Jacksonville, Sanford, Orlando and Lakeland, Florida.

On its way back to Erwin, the train called on more communities, including Ocala, Baldwin, Tallahassee, Lake City, Live Oak, Marianna, Chattahoochee and Pensacola, Florida; Brewton, Evergreen, Greenville, Fort Deposit, Auburn and Montgomery, Alabama; West Point, LaGrange, Newnan, Decatur, Covington, Madison, Union Point, Thomson and Atlanta, Georgia; and McCormick, South Carolina. In Pensacola, the magazine wrote, "the train made several short trips for handicapped youngsters, the Pensacola Historical Society and the public, across Escambia Bay to Pace, Florida, and back."

The *Pensacola News*, in its afternoon edition, and the *Pensacola Journal*, in its morning edition, covered the No. 1's arrival with the same zest the steam locomotive had received from Tampa reporters and photographers. For the *Journal*, staff writer Carl Sanders Jr. described the experience in colorful detail:

ABOARD THE OLD NO. 1—Chugging over the rails at 30 m.p.h.—top speed—this 96-year-old steam engine is not much faster than an old yellow dog on a country road.

But that's not the point.

More than 500 passengers are aboard for the fun of it, many of them children who have never ridden a train before, much less a rolling relic.

The ride is free and the windows are open.

The walls inside the cars are lacquered and the bathrooms have aluminum toilets and sinks. Eleven dark green (circa 1930) passenger and two parlor cars sway sideways on the tracks like seasoned sailors on a clipper ship and up front the whistle's blowing.

"SHOO-WHOOP...SHOO-WHOOP," pause, "WHOOP... SHOO-WHOOP." The longs, a short then another long toot signal a crossing ahead. Motorists wave from stopped autos, little boys swimming in Pensacola Bay stare, fishermen farther out in John boats fan the sky with their arms...

More than 1,500 passengers took the trips, most of them families. The engine pulls 35 tons of coal in a gondola. Fireman George Hatcher, 57, stokes the fire while brother, Ed, 60, toots the whistle and works the steam throttle. Both wear pinstriped railroaders' Pointer Brand overalls with matching engineer's caps and red kerchiefs around sweaty necks.

For many Clinchfield employees, the Tampa Run was a chance to let their Erwin-based railroad shine. In interviews for this book, George Hatcher and retired carman Everette Allen fondly recalled the long excursion. "It was some show," Allen said. "That whole Florida trip, anywhere we went, in all these little towns, there were people lined up to see it." And Hatcher added, "The trip to Florida was a way to glorify the railroad and show some goodwill toward the people, and it was amazing. People would quit working if they were mowing the yard or painting a house or doing whatever, they'd quit right then and there, and rush over to watch and wave at the train." Bob Likens spoke emotionally about the trip for Sally Jackson's oral history project, saying:

The whole trip was for public relations work. What they did at different cities or towns, they would line up children from children's hospitals, orphan homes and then some grade schools, and we would pick up 600 students in one town and take them to the next town. Unload them. Pick up 600 more. And they came in wheelchairs. They came on crutches. They came in—bless their hearts—every shape in the world, [every] deformity you could think of. We even had some come on stretchers. And, we would load them up and take them for a little ride…We would stay there for maybe a day and make two or three or four trips up and down the line to give everybody a chance to ride. But to see those youngsters who had never probably seen a steam engine before, much less ride behind one…Bless their little hearts, you couldn't help feel sorry for them. But when Ed Hatcher, the engineer, would blow the whistle, and the steam would start, smoke would start rolling and we'd start moving, they would scream and holler with delight, and I tell you, the most hardened railroad man would get a lump in his throat just to look at those beautiful little faces.

The public, too, took the excursion to heart, as detailed in the *Family Lines* magazine's conclusion to the "Time Machine" article:

Many nice letters have been received by our System since July. Mrs. Louise B. Lambe, coordinator of volunteer services at the Sunland Center, Marianna, Florida, wrote: "On behalf of our center, may I extend heartfelt thanks for the train ride from Marianna to DeFuniak Springs which your system gave our clients. This ride was a great treat. Many had never taken a train ride before. Please express our thanks to all who helped in any way to make this such a joyous day for us."

16
SHORT TALES FROM THE RAILS

The following is a collection of interesting facts, observations and tales from the good ol' days when the Clinchfield No. 1 rode the rails.

Political Power

Did the No. 1 have the magical touch for politicians? Three Tennessee politicians who rode the No. 1's excursions—Howard Baker Jr., Fred Thompson and Lamar Alexander—were elected as U.S. senators, and all three ran for president, too. Two men—Alexander and Richard W. Riley of South Carolina—were elected governor after campaigning with the No. 1, and both Alexander and Riley also served as U.S. secretary of education. Alexander was appointed by President George H.W. Bush and Riley by President Bill Clinton.

Power Breakfast

Clinchfield No. 1 engineer Ed Hatcher was known for his good humor and quick retorts. His brother George recalled this scene at a Marion, North Carolina restaurant, where the train's crew was eating before getting ready for another day on the rails. The men had ordered country ham and gravy. "Well," George said, "the lady gave us a plastic fork. Well, Ed, first thing, broke his fork in that ham. I told him, 'Well, go ask for another fork,' and he did."

Left: Kelly Carey, Lisa Tilson and Robin Ingle were students at Erwin's Martin Chapel Elementary School in the 1970s, when students got a chance to take one of the Clinchfield No. 1's excursions. *Courtesy of the Robin Ingle Veitch Collection.*

Below: Future South Carolina governor Richard Riley, facing camera, was one of many politicians who took advantage of the Clinchfield No. 1's visit to Georgetown County in May 1978. *Photo by Mary A. Cagle.*

When Ed asked for a replacement, the waitress said, "What did you with the other one?"

"I broke it," he said.

"Well," the waitress replied, "how did you break it?"

And without missing a beat, Ed said, "It got stuck in the gravy."

Number One with a Bullet

The Clinchfield No. 1 was used on the cover of a 1970 album titled *Train Time*, by the Toe River Valley Boys. One album track is called "The Clinchfield Special" and even includes a recording of the No. 1's famous whistle. One of the musicians was Clarence H. Greene, editor of the *Tri-County News* in Spruce Pine, North Carolina, who had been a strong Clinchfield supporter. The photo shoot featuring the No. 1 and the six members of the group was set in Erwin for January 18, 1970, with approval from Clinchfield general manager T.D. Moore. In his letter requesting the use of the No. 1, Greene wrote, "I believe if you could arrange to 'fire up' No. 1 in front of the depot with two or three coaches behind her, this would make a very striking scene. We will hope for sunshine and good weather, of course." On the letter, Moore made a handwritten note and forwarded to his staff, with these directions: "Take care of them...and arrange."

A Rose by Any Other Name

The Clinchfield No. 1 has gone by many names, but perhaps the most loving of them all is "Rosebud." Stories differ on how the engine acquired the name.

In 1970, Bill Cannon claimed chief mechanical officer P.O. Likens once affectionately said, "That's my Rosebud." His wife, Nora, however, noted, "I'm the only Rosebud for Percy."

Another story still passed around by railroaders says the nickname stuck after Likens once again, this time on November 30, 1972, likened the steam engine to a rose. It was the first night after pulling the Baker Special, U.S. senator Howard Baker Jr.'s whistle-stop campaign across Tennessee. Likens, Ed and George Hatcher and two railroad detectives named Bob White and David Crockett had just finished eating dinner at the Hyatt Regency in Knoxville when Likens stood up and said, "I've got to go check on Rosebud." After that, the name stuck.

Idol Worship

After the No. 1 visited the Lowcountry of South Carolina, the *Georgetown Times*, in its March 9, 1978 issue, declared that the Hatcher brothers had set forth a new type of hero worship for local children. "Lots of times, some of the lucky tykes get to climb up into the engine and hang onto the handles and levers themselves," the newspaper wrote. "This could start another generation of idolizing engineers to compare with spacemen, cowboys and fire chiefs.

Dr. Robert Harper, a well-known physician in Andrews, South Carolina, showed up in period costume for the Clinchfield No. 1's visit to Georgetown County in 1978. *Photo by Mary A. Cagle.*

Clean Air Act

The Clinchfield Railroad had to ask the North Carolina Air and Water Quality Committee for a variance for the No. 1's pillars of coal-burned smoke to be released through the hills, valleys and mountains. The state board granted the request without opposition.

Pen Pals

Transportation assistant John Lukianoff made sure customers received polite replies to inquiries. Here's a nice letter from April 21, 1970, from Bob Paval of Cleveland, Ohio: "Dear sir, During the latter part of May, my new wife and I expect to be in the Tennessee area on our honeymoon. I am wondering if you would happen to have any trips scheduled using your famous #1 locomotive, the rebuilt 4-6-0, while we will be there. I would appreciate anything you could tell me. Thank you."

Lukianoff replied with a list of three excursions, May 2, 17 and 24, and added, "Congratulations!!!! May you enjoy the best of everything in your new life."

C.T. McArthur of Birmingham, Alabama, asked on April 21, 1970, "Please advise us which in your opinion would be the most desirable from the standpoint of scenic beauty of any trips you may have planned."

Lukianoff replied: "Actually, both ends of our railroad have some exceptional scenery and it would be difficult to say which is best. It all depends on an individual's point of view."

Transportation assistant John Lukianoff and chief mechanical officer P.O. Likens (center and in ties) pose with 1969 uniformed car marshals (from left) A.J. "Alf" Peoples, Sam Tittle, Brice Kerns and Jerry Keasling. *Courtesy of the Bob Likens Collection.*

Standing at far left, J.L. Lonon, who served as an agent/operator, dispatcher, trainmaster and superintendent during forty-four years with the Clinchfield Railroad, poses with excursion passengers. *Courtesy of Chris Lonon.*

"Cashing" in on Publicity

In 1974, music superstar Johnny Cash hosted an ABC television special titled *Ridin' the Rails: The Great American Train Story*, an hour-long documentary that featured video of the Clinchfield No. 1 speeding along with its bell clanging. "You know there's nothing that stirs my imagination like the sound of a steam locomotive," Cash said.

Looking So Young

Following a 1974 chartered excursion by the Bluegrass Model Railroad Club that brought fans from twenty-three states to ride and included a stop at the Breaks Interstate Park in Virginia, Carl Adkins jokingly questioned, in his newsletter column "The Headlight" how the ancient No. 1 could still operate in such a grand fashion. "Do you believe," he asked, "that they give the One Spot a bottle of Geritol every time they water her, to keep it so young?"

Underground Railroad

There were fifty-five tunnels on the 277-mile Clinchfield route, the longest being the Sandy Ridge at 7,854 feet. The train spent so much time in the tunnels, it's been called the "Clinchfield Subway."

Six-year-old Tony King waves from the No. 1 in 1978. A fourth-generation railroader, King is now an engineer for CSX. *Photo by Hobart Laws, courtesy of Tony and Susan King.*

A Right Smart Chameleon

The Clinchfield did such a good job disguising the diesel helpers that assisted the No. 1 that many passengers never knew they existed. Bill Cannon told this story in *Trains* magazine in 1972: "Often people ask why the railroad carries 'baggage cars' (the disguised diesels) on an excursion train, and the Clinchfield crewmen reply with a grin that they 'have to carry lunch somewhere.' Outsiders have been known to think that No. 1 does all the work, and the proud Clinchfield men let the illusion stand."

Coming and Going

Approximately 42 percent of the Clinchfield Railroad's main line is on curve because of the mountain terrain, but for an excursion train, this bendable view allows passengers to see themselves coming and going, so to speak.

Job Duties

The Hatcher brothers, while both engineers, never switched duties while working with the No. 1. "Ed might bend my shovel," George told *Sandlapper* magazine in 1971, "and he's afraid I might mess up his whistle."

Lights, Camera, Action

A Hollywood film crew booked passage on the No. 1 in 1970 to scout for places to shoot *Christy*. "We pass through some of the most beautiful country in the world…They were astonished," T.D. Moore recalled. "They said they never knew anything like this existed east of the Rockies."

Paper Route

The Clinchfield No. 1 delivered more than passengers. The steam engine would make regular stops when passing through the remote Lost Cove area of North Carolina to deliver a load of newspapers at a cabin occupied by Carl and Dora Cooper. In 1969, the couple had lived on the hillside for twenty-seven years. The railroad's newspaper delivery was the couple's only contact with the outside world, as they didn't own a television or radio.

Catching a Wave

"Miss Bonnie," as she was known to railroaders, spent a lifetime waving as trains pounded by her North Carolina home near Hankins Crossing. She waved enthusiastically, and the engineers and crew did the same back. At Christmas, train crews were known to stop and deliver gifts to their friend, but in September 1970, the crew of the No. 1 did something special—took "Miss Bonnie" and two friends on a free ride on the Clinchfield Special. It was, she told reporters, the "ride of a lifetime."

A Way with Words

Maybe it was the time, but newspaper reporters seemed to write with more flair than they do today. Here's some of the best:

William D. McDonald of the *State*: "Old Number One crept like a sassy snake through the Blue Ridge Mountain scene which was dotted with the familiar hillside hamlets...Gray smoke puffed from the engine's stack and trailed behind like a gray bridal veil."

Dot Jackson of the *Charlotte Observer*: "Old folks come out on the porches to wave. 'Give 'em two longs, a short and a long,' said Ed. You pull an ancient braided rope, and the whip-poor-will sings, 'Whoooo—Whoooo—WhoWhooooeeeeeeeooooo.'"

The *Charlotte Observer* (writer not listed): "Wouldn't you know that, right in the middle of the jet age, somebody would rediscover steam railway engines?"

Ellis Simon of the *Greenville News*: "The Clinchfield carries people because it likes people, but the railroad likes people because Clinchfield people like people."

Susan Dodge of the *Spartanburg Herald*: "Photographers sat on the railroad track. Cameras all a-shutter. Along came the choo-choo. Clickety clack. Snap. Click. Snap. Click. It was the Clinchfield Railroad Company's steam engine...hissing and clanging, bringing 600 people from Johnson City and Erwin, Tennessee, to Spartanburg for lunch."

Jack Lauterer of the *Charlotte Observer*: "There's a hint of a wail, a lonesome moan in the wind somewhere...You hold your breath and hear it once more and you're sure of it. Around the bend, clipping time in half, chuffs the Clinchfield Special, a real coal-eating steam engine."

17

A LETTER FROM NO. 1

This "Letter from No. 1" (actually written by assistant chief dispatcher James F. Garner) was sent ahead to other railroad divisions before the start of the No. 1's trip to Tampa, Florida, in 1978, as an introduction and how-to guide, as many workers on the other lines had never worked with a steam engine:

Hello there,

I am Clinchfield No. 1, jaunty little 4-6-0 steam engine off the Clinchfield Railroad with B-unit helpers and train. I usually spend most of my time on the Clinchfield handling excursion trains through the mountains and occasionally I go off the Clinchfield for special appearances. And this is one of the occasions, and we will be operating over your division real soon at thirty-five miles per hour.

Oh-oh, I thought I saw a frown, and some question marks and hear some mumbling: thirty-five mph, no coal chutes, water tanks. What about my hot-shot trains and train operation on my hot-shot division? What in the world am I going to do with a steam engine, etc, etc, etc? Well, let me set you at ease. At thirty-five mph, I'm real good in getting in and out of sidings, dodging the hot shots as I do it all the time at home on the Clinchfield. And on secondary or branch lines, you won't even know I am around!

Since I do not do a lot of real hard work, it doesn't take a lot of coal or water, and one of the B-units can carry extra water for me. I usually have a car of coal preceding me or with me. Takes a clamshell full to round coal pile off on tender (maybe 2) when I tie up for the day, along

The East Tennessee chapter of the National Railway Historical Society used this artwork on fliers for its Clinchfield No. 1 excursions in the 1970s. *Courtesy of East Tennessee State University's Archives of Appalachia.*

with water hose for tender. I need to be tied up where I can be viewed by the public and where I will not interfere with other operations, where safety may be exercised.

When my coaches are used will also require water and ice for water coolers, and on rear of train, parlor car White Oak is air-conditioned (ice-activated) side bunkers and usually requires twelve to fourteen 100-pound blocks of ice each day, also water. This should be done prior to start of trips in the morning to save delay.

When I tie up, I will require engine watchmen (if possible, one familiar with steam engines), or responsible person, usually a laborer to keep water in my boiler and feed me to keep steam up, no hard chore, just tender love and care.

My helpers are two F-7 B-units, and after long a deadhead trip or several days of operation will require about 1,000 gallons fuel per unit and maybe a little water and day prior to long deadhead trip to top fuel tanks off. B-units are operated from control panel in my cab.

Traveling along with me, Ed and George Hatcher (brothers and veteran CRR enginemen). Ed runs me and just keeps me tingly all over when he blows my whistle. George also feeds me, keeps me in water so I can make plenty of steam and smoke, and he is also a whistle-blowing fireman, as I have two whistles, which is also unusual. Also, Mr. P.O. Likens, retired chief mechanical officer for the Clinchfield (my Papa), and two mechanical foremen from Clinchfield mechanical department go with me and keep me serviced and pretty and keep up with supplies, fuel, water, etc. And keep me well, so I don't get any ailments. I usually have some other Clinchfield supervisory personnel along to make sure all goes well. My entire crew requires good food and lodging and, being from the mountains, really likes seafood.

While on SCL, I usually require trainmaster and road foreman of engines along with full passenger crew (engineman, fireman, conductor, brakeman and flagman) dressed casual. For something special, conductors wear ties, as suits full of cinders, coal smoke, along with a little rain, are hard to clean. Denim outfits, overalls, SCL blue denim hats are right smart—and fit right in with my train. Trainmaster and road foreman of engines usually coordinate movements and local train operation wherever I operate.

When I handle people, safety cannot be overemphasized. My coaches have a unique type of air conditioning, raise windows when hot, lower them when cold. Each window has a safe latch when secured properly. Passengers must keep arms, heads inside of windows. Some of the vestibule doors are dutch-style ½ doors, top may be opened, but do not hang out the openings. Other doors that are full doors must be kept closed when train is moving, and only opened by train personnel or to detrain or entrain passengers.

Conductor, flagman or designated party must be on observation platform of White Oak at all times when train is moving for safety and do not let any one sit or hang over the railing, conductors, etc patrol train to enforce safety. People should remain seated until train stops to get off. I have a real good safety record and your personal attention will keep it that way. Keep safety in mind all the time with courtesy.

When I am hauling, passengers will need a couple of EMTs or medics with supplies on board (Re: motion sickness, heat, nausea) are invaluable when a lot of people involved. In loading and unloading, passengers will need assistance from crew unless otherwise provided and caution must be used entraining and detraining passengers using step boxes and especially those real young and elderly.

And in speaking of hot shots, while handling people, please treat me like a "Hot Shot," especially in hot weather, taking in consideration my unique air conditioning, I spoke of. After all, I came from mountains. I need to be dispatched promptly with little delay as possible to myself or other trains, movements, coordinated with chief dispatcher, dispatcher, trainmaster and road foreman of engines complete with mutual understanding with everyone's full cooperation, no problems.

In the sea of faces of those who come to see me and ride, there is usually some of our customers and influential people, along with the media. And the great wealth of publicity I get will be very valuable asset to Family Lines for many years to come.

After seeing the enjoyment of people's faces, heard the comments, and the coal smoke has settled and the whistle has echoed away, you will say that was real nice, everything went smoothly and you had a part in it and a glimpse at a vanishing breed of Americana Railroadiana, and you will be a friend of mine, and I will have enjoyed being on your division. And the result, I have never seen a smoother operation or a better division, and I have traveled a lot of divisions.

Sincerely in Steam and Safety,
No. 1

EPILOGUE

No other engine in history has had so much attention or been held in such high esteem.
—William S. "Bill" Cannon

It went out like it came in: via Spartanburg, South Carolina. On January 8, 1969, the Clinchfield No. 1 chugged down from Erwin to the railroad's most southern destination on the Clinchfield Railroad line to announce passenger service was restored in the way of special excursion trains. Then, on May 5, 1979, one last excursion made its way to that same city. A little more than a decade separated the two bookended Spartanburg dates, clinched together by thousands of miles under the No. 1's still-shiny black metal and gleaming brass belt. An entire calendar year of excursions had already been planned, but they were quickly and unceremoniously abandoned. It was an abrupt end to years of happy days.

Times were changing at the Clinchfield Railroad. The Family Lines corporate office was no longer interested in T.D. Moore's mix of nostalgia and business, and Moore was removed from his job of eleven years and replaced by J.W. Thomas until Family Lines itself was no more, swallowed whole by CSX Transportation.

If Moore's experiment was cut short, it in no way diminishes the success of the project or his vision. The excursions never lost money and had, as the general manager with the million-dollar smile always predicted, brought fame and goodwill to the railroad business. Never before—or since—has a railroad received so much positive press, good word of mouth and downright love and adoration.

A beautiful photo of the Clinchfield No. 1 and its coal tender at night in Knoxville, Tennessee, in 1978. *Photo by Dennis W. Hetzner. Courtesy of the David Crockett Collection.*

With the excursions now halted and the locomotive no longer of use to the corporate-minded, back-to-business-as-usual Family Lines, the Clinchfield No. 1 was sent to the B&O Railroad Museum in Baltimore, Maryland. The locomotive is a shiny star there, proudly displayed in the roundhouse beside relics of the B&O past. Visitors can climb aboard the No. 1, touch and pull on the same levers the Hatcher brothers used to pilot it up and down Appalachian mountains. Even the museum's gift shop pays reverence to its mountain engine with a No. 1 replica serving as a shelf.

Everette Allen, who came to work for the Clinchfield in 1967 at the age of twenty-one, was the last Clinchfielder to ride the No. 1, as it left Erwin for Baltimore, not under its own steam but towed along by a diesel engine that had long ago given deference to its nearly one-hundred-year-old cousin, now once again a machine of a bygone era. Allen, eventually retiring from the railroad in 1999 as a supervisor, had worked aboard the excursion train for seven years.

"I was on the trips to Memphis. I was on the trip to Florida. About everywhere that train went, I was on it," he said. "My job was to look over the mechanical parts. We did all the painting when we would stop. We would do all the painting, greasing and oil and stuff on it and when it stopped."

After almost every excursion, the duty to touch up No. 1's makeup—that is, its silver face—fell to Allen and company. "Every night, she got a fresh coat of silver aluminum paint," Allen said. "I can't begin to tell you how much paint we used over the years. We kept gallons and gallons of it for every excursion. She was so hot from being on the rails, the paint dried quickly. There was no worry about the paint not drying. None at all."

So when it came time for the No. 1 to head out for retirement, it was Allen who was in charge of taking it north to Kentucky, where the engine would receive another transfer to Maryland. "I was the last one," Allen said, "who rode the No. 1 out of Erwin, the very last man…When it was going to the museum, I actually rode it and I did the oil and greasing. She was completely towed, but she still had to have oil and grease."

Looking back, Allen isn't sure why he was the man chosen for the job, other than because he "worked hard" and "always got the job done." "After I started working the excursions, I don't know one I wasn't on," he said, "so when it came for it very last trip out of Erwin, it felt like a real honor."

When Allen arrived in Corbin, Kentucky, with the No. 1, he was met by Fred Miracle, who took over the responsibility of the No. 1 from that point. And but for a few brief and short excursions at the Baltimore museum, the Clinchfield No. 1 has never been on the rails again. A "Miracle" made sure it got to Baltimore safely, but it was love that made it so special to so many people.

For George Hatcher, the excursions are some of the happiest days of his life. Only a few months after the company ceased the operations, his brother, Ed, the much-loved engineer, died, a victim to the cancer he'd fought even while running the No. 1. "I really do miss those days," he said in a 2014 interview in which he also talked about dreams of seeing the little locomotive return to Erwin. "If enough people got together, we could. I would like to have that engine where schoolchildren could come and look at it and ask questions about it right here in Erwin. I would love to tell them why it's called an iron horse or a choo-choo train."

Nancy Moore Pearson isn't surprised her father's vision in 1968 still resonates with people even today. "When people have good motives and want to do something positive, whatever it is they do, whatever action it is they take often becomes bigger than what was ever intended," she said, "because good attracts good and positive, actually, attracts positive."

And, for so many people, they can still hear that whistle blow through the valleys and up, high, to the mountaintops. It will always be No. 1—Rosebud, the One Spot, the Clinchfield No. 1.

ABOUT THE AUTHORS

Mark A. Stevens and A.J. "Alf" Peoples met only a few years ago in Erwin, Tennessee. Mark was publisher of the *Erwin Record*, the town's hard-hitting, award-winning weekly newspaper, and Alf was an engineer for CSX. They first got together when Mark was penning an article for his newspaper about the Clinchfield No. 1. The two have been friends ever since.

Authors A.J. "Alf" Peoples and Mark A. Stevens pose with Clinchfield Passenger Car 100 in March 2014 at the North Carolina Transportation Museum.

In 2013, the two authored a limited-edition pictorial history book titled *The One & Only: A Pictorial History of the Clinchfield No. 1*. The Knoxville, Tennessee–based East Tennessee Historical Society named the book a recipient of its 2014 Award of Distinction for "excellence in preserving the region's history."

Mark is a native of Hampton, Tennessee, and the son of Amos and Peggy Stevens. He graduated from East Tennessee State University in 1991 with a bachelor's degree in communications and a minor in history. He has served as an editor at daily and weekly newspapers in Tennessee and Louisiana and been the publisher of two: the *Record*, from 1997 until 2011, and the *Elizabethton Star*, from 2012 until 2014. He has received regional, state and national awards for news, feature and editorial writing, as well as top awards for his humor column.

In addition *to The One & Only*, Stevens is the author of *Then & Now: Unicoi County* and *Welcome to Erwin: Where the Mayor's Name Is Bubba and Main Street's a Dead End*. He has served as editor for two books, O. Ray Knapp's *Legends, Lies & Other Tales: Stories from Flag Pond & the Mountains of Northeast Tennessee* and *Charging the Dome: 2011 Ragin' Cajuns Bring It Home*.

Stevens is president of his own publishing and marketing company, MAS*communications*. He lives in Pawley's Island,

Author Mark A. Stevens on September 18, 2013, with the Clinchfield No. 1 at the B&O Railroad Museum in Baltimore, Maryland. *Photo by Amy D. Stevens, courtesy of B&O Railroad Museum.*

South Carolina, with his wife, the former Amy Dickeson of Jonesborough, Tennessee, and their dog, Rue.

Alf is a third-generation railroader who grew up to work on both steam and diesel engines for the Clinchfield Railroad. The son of Jack and Ruth Peoples, he was born in Erwin, not too far from the railroad that would shape his entire life.

He went to work for the Clinchfield Railroad in 1969 as a Clinchfield No. 1 car marshal and was soon promoted to captain. He has worked as a brakeman, conductor and fireman. Today, he is a locomotive engineer for CSX Transportation and follows the same route he did when serving with the Clinchfield No. 1 crew.

Alf is past secretary and president of Division 781 of the Brotherhood of Locomotive Engineers. He serves on the board of directors for the Unicoi County Heritage Museum and the Clinchfield Railroad Museum. He is a

In 2013, Alf Peoples presented ninety-three-year-old George Hatcher, fireman for the Clinchfield No. 1, with a copy of the book *The One & Only: A Pictorial History of the Clinchfield No. 1*. *Photo by Bobby Knight.*

member of the Carolina-Clinchfield and Watauga Valley chapters of the National Railway Historical Society.

Alf lives in Johnson City, Tennessee, and is the proud father of Sarah Peoples Mullins and grandfather of Jackson Neil Mullins.

Visit us at
www.historypress.net
....
This title is also available as an e-book